What's on the Menu

Shazia Khan

Foreword
Sanjeev Kapoor

Om Books International

Reprinted in 2024

Om Books International

Corporate & Editorial Office
A-12, Sector 64, Noida 201 301
Uttar Pradesh, India
Phone: +91 120 477 4100
Email: editorial@ombooks.com
Website: www.ombooksinternational.com

Sales Office
107, Ansari Road, Darya Ganj
New Delhi 110 002, India
Phone: +91 11 4000 9000
Email: sales@ombooks.com
Website: www.ombooks.com

Editor: Ipshita Mitra
Design & Layout: Shraboni Roy

Food photography: Saina Jayapal
Food styling and image processing: Farrukh Aziz Ansari
Cover & section opening images: Chef Sarabjeet Singh
Cover & section opening images (shoot location): Slurp Studio

ISBN: 978-93-85609-60-2

Printed in India

10 9 8 7 6 5 4 3 2

contents

Foreword

Passion. Dedication. These were the two qualities of Shazia Khan that impressed me the most when I met her for the first time on the sets of *MasterChef India* Season 2. She came with a wealthy legacy of cooking skills inherited from her family of fantastic cooks and great hosts. Interestingly, she had not undergone any formal training and it was her love for cooking that brought her to *MasterChef India*.

The show put her through the grind and she faced many challenges as a contestant. She never crumbled under pressure and came out with a smile on her face at the end of each and every test. It was here that I watched her grow as a chef as she continued to polish her culinary techniques. She never let criticism dampen her spirit; instead, she used it to better her skills. Gradually, her creativity peaked and nothing could distract her from achieving her goal.

Shazia's relationship with food is remarkable. She has cooking on her mind all the time. Whatever she may be doing, she is always thinking recipes. This level of commitment is rare and it has stood her in good stead.

What's on the Menu is a delightful compilation of the recipes of her favourite dishes. Shazia's kitchen secrets, ideas and innovations are worth emulating. The 90 recipes in this collection have been prepared with easily available ingredients and if, for some reason, you are unsure, Shazia provides you with the next best substitute that guarantees no change in the taste of the dish. She is one of those few chefs who prefers to stay away from too many complexities while making delicious food. One of my favourites is Dal Gosht with Brown Rice; it is not only rich in taste and flavour, the dish has high nutritional value as well.

Shazia and I have one common trait—both of us swear by the most important ingredient in any dish—LOVE. With that belief under her hat, she can only work magic. Good luck and best wishes to Shazia and *What's on the Menu*.

Sanjeev Kapoor

Introduction

Cooking has always been a grand event (celebration) through my growing up years in a joint family. I am fortunate that even after my marriage, I was able to carry forward this legacy. Deeply inspired by my father, mother, grandmother, and later, my mother-in-law—wonderful cooks and fantastic hosts—my home turned into my little culinary haven, where I greatly enjoyed treating family and friends to sumptuous meals.

My journey from being a housewife to a chef has been a fulfilling one. While I never had any formal training, I did not stop experimenting with recipes. It was always trial and error in the kitchen. Initially, it would take me a few bad rounds to arrive at the perfect dish but failures have never disheartened me. I was always willing to keep trying and keep growing. In this pursuit of perfection, an opportunity to participate in *MasterChef India* Season 2, came my way. The show allowed me to dream big in the culinary world. Soon, I began to feel more confident in my cooking innovations. From the very first dish—Custard with Fruits—which I prepared often as a child, to rustling up dishes that received favourable reviews, playing with flavours and textures, combining unusual ingredients and coming up with unusual ways of presentation, it's been a rewarding transformation for me.

Modern Indian cooking is all about fusion and that is what I have tried to achieve through my recipes in *What's on the Menu*. Readers can tweak these recipes and add elements to make them their own. We must remember that simplicity is the key to a delicious dish.

My all-time favourite ingredient is garlic. However, nothing can parallel the one ingredient that completes every dish—LOVE.

Special Ingredients

*For the Special Garam Masala Powder

Nutmeg (*jaiphal*) 1 (grated)
Clove (*laung*) 3
Cinnamon (*dalchini*) 10 gms
Cardamom (*elaichi*) 20 pods
Black cardamom (*badi elaichi*) 3 pods
Mace (*javitri*) petals 4
Coriander (*dhania*) seeds 50 gms
Cumin (*jeera*) seeds 50 gms
Black peppercorns 1 tbsp

Grind all the ingredients into a powder. Store in an airtight container and use as required.

*For the Garam Masala Powder

Cinnamon (*dalchini*) 30 gms
Clove (*laung*) 2 tbsp
Cardamom (*elaichi*) 2 tbsp

Grind all the ingredients into a powder. Store in an airtight container and use as required.

*Method for Preparing the Red Chilli Paste

Boil 100 grams of long, dry red chillies (*Kashmiri*). Allow them to cool down and strain them. Add ½ tsp salt and grind into a smooth paste. Store in the freezer and use as required.

*Method for Preparing the Fresh Coconut Milk

To extract fresh coconut milk, grate the flesh of 2 coconuts. Soak the grated coconut with 2 cups of warm water for 15 minutes. Blend in a grinder and strain through a muslin cloth. Repeat the process thrice. The first round will give the thicker extract. Gradually, by the last round, you will get the thinner extract.

*Method for Preparing the Chilli Oil

Mix 1 tablespoon of chilli flakes, 1 tablespoon of red chilli powder and ½ teaspoon of salt in a heatproof cup. Heat ½ cup of oil in a small pan. When hot, pour the oil over the chilli flake mix. Set aside to cool down and strain. Store in a bottle and use as required.

Soups

Carrot, Lentil and Saffron
Soup with Dukkah Spice 13

Broccoli and Spinach Soup with Corn 14

Lemongrass Rasam 17

Asian Vegetable and Rice Soup 18

Tomato, Beetroot Soup with Grilled
Pepper and Basil Crostini 21

Peas, Parmesan and Thyme Soup 22

Chicken and Oats Shorba 25

Chicken Balls, Rice Noodles with
Spicy Coconut Broth 26

Roasted Pumpkin and
Chicken Soup 29

Gosht Ka Sherwa 30

Spicy Prawn Soup 33

This is a simple, nourishing soup. The saffron brings in a subtle flavour and adds a lovely colour to the soup. What makes this dish warm and delicious is the crunchiness that comes from the dukkah spice. Dukkah is an Egyptian spice mix made with nuts and herbs.

Carrot, Lentil and Saffron Soup with Dukkah Spice

Serves: 6

Ingredients

Butter 1 tbsp	Water 2 cups
Carrot 2 (peeled & sliced)	Saffron (*kesar*) ½ tsp (soaked in a little warm milk)
Onion 1 (thinly sliced)	Salt to taste
Garlic 5 cloves	Black pepper powder ½ tsp
Red lentils (*masoor dal*) ¼ cup	Hung curd 4 tbsp
*Vegetable stock 2 cups	

Method

- In a large saucepan, heat the butter. Add the carrots, along with onion and garlic. Sauté for 3 minutes, until onions are translucent.
- Add the red lentils and sauté for a minute.
- Next, add the vegetable stock and water. Cook till the lentils and carrots are tender.
- After this mixture cools down, blend it into a purée in batches until smooth. Add water, if necessary, to achieve the desired consistency.
- Pour the purée into the saucepan, add the saffron and bring to a boil.
- Season with salt and black pepper powder. Pour the soup into a bowl, place a quenelle of hung curd at the centre and sprinkle the dukkah spice. Serve.

For the Dukkah Spice Mix

Pistachios 2 tbsp	Cumin (*jeera*) seeds 1 tsp
Sesame (*til*) seeds 1 tsp	Fennel (*saunf*) seeds ½ tsp

Method

- In a preheated pan, on low flame, add the pistachios and roast for 2 minutes.
- Add the remaining ingredients and roast for another minute.
- Transfer the mixture onto a plate and let it cool.
- Grind the mixture coarsely, in a food processor.

* For the vegetable stock recipe, refer to page no. 18

Broccoli and Spinach Soup with Corn

Serves: 6

Ingredients

Butter 2 tbsp
Onion 1 (thinly sliced)
Green chilli 2
Garlic 5 cloves
Broccoli florets 200 gms
*Vegetable stock 1 cup
Milk 2 cups
Spinach leaves 100 gms
Corn kernels ½ cup (boiled)
Lemon juice 1 tbsp
Salt to taste
Chilli flakes ½ tbsp (to garnish)

Method

- In a pan, heat the butter. Add onion, chillies, garlic, broccoli and sauté for 3 minutes.
- Add the vegetable stock and milk. Cook till the broccoli is done. (Make sure you don't overcook the broccoli.)
- Add the spinach leaves and boil for another minute.
- Remove the mixture from the fire and keep aside to cool down.
- Transfer the mixture into a blender and prepare a purée till you get a smooth consistency. Add extra milk if needed.
- Pour the purée into a saucepan and bring to a boil.
- Add the corn kernels, lemon juice and season with salt.
- Garnish with chilli flakes.
- Serve.

* For the vegetable stock recipe, refer to page no. 18

Broccoli and spinach are two of the least favourite vegetables and this soup recipe guarantees to bust that myth. Filled with goodness, this easy-to-make soup will soothe your taste buds and leave you craving for more. The play of spices, together with the crispness of corn makes this soup a bestselling dish.

Being a South Indian, I love my rasam, especially the kind that my mum makes. I have given this recipe a delicious twist by adding lemongrass. This exotic ingredient lends a unique flavour to the dish, making it an instant favourite in my family.

Lemongrass Rasam

Serves: 6

Ingredients

Pigeon peas (*Toor dal / arhar dal*) ½ cup
Onion 1 (diced)
Tomato 2 (diced)
Tamarind (*imli*) 15 gms (1 small ball)
Water 4 cups
Roasted papad to serve

For the Spice Mix

Fresh coriander (*dhania*) leaves 15 gms
Black peppercorns 1 tsp
Cumin (*jeera*) seeds 1 tsp
Garlic 8 cloves

For the Tempering

Oil 1 tbsp
Dried red chilli 3 (broken into two halves)
Curry leaves 7
Lemongrass 2 stalks (crushed)
Salt to taste

Method

- Pressure cook the dal, onion, tomatoes and tamarind with water for about 3 whistles.
- Strain the dal water and keep aside.
- Coarsely crush the coriander leaves, peppercorns, cumin seeds and garlic in a food processor to make the spice mix.
- In a pan, heat the oil. Add the dried chillies, curry leaves and the spice mix. Add the strained dal water and season with salt.
- Add the lemongrass stalks. Reduce flame and simmer till the flavour of lemongrass is infused in the rasam.
- Strain the mixture.
- Serve with roasted papad.

Asian Vegetable and Rice Soup

Serves: 6

Ingredients

- Oil 2 tbsp
- Star anise 2
- Ginger 1-inch (very finely chopped)
- Garlic 1 tsp (very finely chopped)
- *Red chilli paste 1 tsp
- Long grain / Basmati rice ¼ cup (washed & soaked for 15 minutes)
- **Vegetable stock 4 cups
- Mixed vegetables 250 gms (sliced) (baby corn, mushroom, broccoli florets, carrot, snow peas)
- Soya sauce 2 tsp
- Vinegar 1 tsp
- Sugar 1 tsp
- Salt to taste
- Sesame (*til*) oil ¼ tsp

Method

- In a pan, heat the oil. Add star anise, ginger, garlic, red chilli paste and sauté for 30 seconds to one minute.
- Add the soaked rice and sauté for another minute.
- Add the stock and bring to a boil till the rice is half cooked.
- Add the vegetables (add the snow peas in the end) and simmer, till the rice is fully cooked and the vegetables are tender but crisp.
- Add soya sauce, vinegar, sugar and salt.
- Add the sesame oil before serving.

**For the Basic Vegetable Stock

- Onion 2 (quartered with skin)
- Garlic 8 cloves (crushed with skin)
- Ginger 1-inch (roughly sliced)
- Celery 2 stalks (roughly chopped with leaves)
- Leek 2 stalks (stems roughly chopped)
- Carrot 2 (peeled & sliced)
- Potato 1 (diced with skin)
- Cauliflower florets 200 gms
- Bay leaf (*tej patta*) 2
- Whole black peppercorns 1 tsp
- Water 2 litres

Method

- In a large pot, combine and mix all the ingredients in 2 litres of water.
- Bring to a boil, and allow to simmer for 45 minutes.
- Remove from heat, strain and use as required.

*For the red chilli paste recipe, refer to page no. 9

Star anise is the actual hero of this dish. Its flavour combines well with the added rice and this makes the soup a wholesome meal by itself.

As a kid, I always loved savouring a bowl of tomato soup. In this recipe, I have introduced beetroot that not only helps dilute the tanginess of the tomatoes, but also lends the dish a pretty colour.

Tomato, Beetroot Soup with Grilled Pepper and Basil Crostini

Serves: 6

Ingredients

- Butter 2 tbsp
- Olive oil 1 tbsp
- Bay leaf (*tej patta*) 1
- Cinnamon (*dalchini*) 1 stick
- Onion 1 (thinly sliced)
- Garlic 5 cloves
- Tomato 5 (quartered)
- Water 4 cups
- Beetroot 1 (peeled & diced)
- Black pepper powder ½ tsp
- Salt to taste
- Cream 4 tbsp
- Black peppercorns to garnish (crushed)

Method

- In a saucepan, heat 1 tablespoon of butter and 1 tablespoon of olive oil.
- Add the bay leaf, cinnamon stick, onion, garlic and tomatoes. Sauté for 2 minutes.
- Add 3 cups of water and bring to a boil. Cook till the tomatoes are soft.
- Once the mixture cools down, blend and strain. Discard the bay leaf and cinnamon stick before blending the soup.
- In a separate pan, sauté the beetroot with the remaining 1 tablespoon of butter. Add one cup of water and cook till the beetroot is done. Once the mixture cools, blend into a purée.
- Transfer the tomato soup to a saucepan and add the beetroot purée. Bring to a boil.
- Season with salt and pepper.
- Serve the soup with a swirl of cream and garnish with freshly-crushed peppercorns.

For the Crostini

- Red bell pepper 1
- Basil (*tulsi*) leaves 10 (finely chopped)
- Olive oil 1 tbsp
- Lemon juice ½ tsp
- Black pepper powder ½ tsp
- Salt to taste
- Baguette 1

Method

- Rub the pepper with a little bit of oil and grill in a preheated oven at 220°C for about 20 minutes, until the skin is charred. Keep aside in a bowl.
- Once the grilled pepper cools down, remove the skin, deseed and cut into small dices.
- In a small bowl, add all the other ingredients to the pepper and mix well.
- Slice the baguette and lightly toast them. Spoon the mixture over these slices and serve.

Peas, Parmesan and Thyme Soup

Serves: 6

Ingredients

Oil 1 tbsp
Onion 1 (sliced)
Carrot 1 (diced)
Leek 1 stalk (stem finely chopped)
Celery 1 stalk (roughly chopped with leaves)
Fresh thyme 8 sprigs
Water 4 cups
Parmesan cheese 50 gms (grated)
Fresh green peas 200 gms (shelled)
Sugar 1 tsp
Salt to taste
White pepper powder ½ tsp
Microgreens of pea shoot to garnish (optional)

Method

- In a saucepan, heat the oil. Add onion, carrot, leek, celery and thyme and sauté till the onion turns translucent. Add water and bring to a rapid boil.
- Add the grated Parmesan into the mixture and simmer for 20 minutes to get a well-flavoured broth. Strain and keep aside.
- Mix the green peas with sugar; add a pinch of salt and some water. Boil till the peas are cooked. Allow to cool and blend to a smooth purée.
- Mix the pea purée with the vegetable broth. Add salt and pepper and simmer the soup for 5 to 6 minutes.
- Portion the prepared soup into a soup bowl.
- Garnish with shavings of Parmesan cheese and microgreens of pea shoot.
- Serve.

This recipe is close to my heart because it was during one of the team challenges on a popular culinary reality show that I, along with fellow contestants, had prepared this soup. I was also appointed the team captain. The experience was enriching and unforgettable. That's why, every time I make this soup, I revisit the good old days.

My family enjoys this soup, especially during Ramadan. Since this soup scores high on nourishment and nutritional benefits, chicken and oats shorba makes for an ideal dish to feast upon during the fasting period.

Chicken and Oats Shorba

Serves: 6

Ingredients

Oil 2 tbsp
Cinnamon (*dalchini*) 1 stick
Onion ½ (finely diced)
Chicken 250 gms (with bones)
Ginger paste 1 tsp
Garlic paste 1 tsp
Turmeric (*haldi*) powder ¼ tsp
Red chilli powder 1 tsp
Tomato purée ½ cup
Curd / yoghurt (*dahi*) 1 tbsp
Lemon juice of ½ a lemon
Water 6 cups
Mint leaves 7
Salt to taste
Oats 5 tbsp

For the Masala Paste

Onion ½ (roughly chopped)
Tomato 1 (roughly chopped)
Fresh coriander (*dhania*) leaves 3 tbsp (chopped)
Green chilli 2

Method

- Blend all the ingredients, needed to prepare the masala paste, into a smooth consistency.
- In a saucepan, heat the oil. Add the cinnamon stick, onion and fry till the onions turn translucent.
- Add the chicken pieces and cook for 3 minutes.
- Add the ginger-garlic pastes and fry for a minute.
- Add the turmeric and red chilli powder.
- Add the masala paste, tomato purée, curd, lemon juice and cook for 5 minutes.
- Pour water, add mint leaves and salt. Cook the broth till the chicken is done.
- Remove the chicken pieces and shred them. Add the shredded chicken pieces back into the broth along with oats.
- Cook till the oats are done and the soup is slightly thick in consistency.
- Serve hot.

Chicken Balls, Rice Noodles with Spicy Coconut Broth

Serves: 6

Ingredients

For the Chicken Balls

- Chicken 150 gms (minced)
- Spring onion 1 stalk (green & white parts finely chopped)
- Garlic paste 1 tsp
- Ginger paste 1 tsp
- Oyster sauce 1 tbsp
- Soya sauce 1 tsp
- Fresh red chilli 1 (very finely chopped)
- Salt to taste

For the Masala Paste

- Coriander (*dhania*) seeds 3 tsp
- Cumin (*jeera*) seeds 1 tsp
- Long, dry red chilli (*Kashmiri*) 5 (soaked in hot water for some time)
- Lemongrass 2 stalks
- Asian shallots (*chhote pyaaz*) 4
- Garlic 6 cloves
- Turmeric (*haldi*) powder ½ tsp
- Oil as required

For the Soup

- Rice vermicelli noodles 100 gms
- Oil 1 tbsp
- *Chicken stock 3 cups
- Coconut milk 200 ml
- Snow peas 50 gms (trimmed & diagonally sliced into half)
- Salt to taste
- Fresh coriander (*dhania*) leaves (a few)
- Lemon wedges to garnish

Method

- In a large bowl, add the minced chicken along with the remaining ingredients to prepare the chicken balls. Mix well. Make small, round balls and keep aside.
- Using a food processor or blender, blend all the masala paste ingredients into a smooth paste. Add cooking oil, as required, to assist blending.
- In a bowl, place the noodles and cover with boiling water. Allow the noodles to soak for 5 minutes or until soft. Drain the noodles and keep aside.
- In a saucepan, heat the oil on low flame. Add the masala paste and stir-fry until fragrant.
- Add the chicken stock and bring to a boil. Drop the chicken balls into the saucepan one after the other. Reduce heat to low flame and simmer for 5 minutes till the chicken balls are done.
- Add the coconut milk, cook for a minute, and then add the snow peas. Season with salt.
- In a soup plate, place the noodles, spoon the soup with the chicken balls over it. Top with snow peas and garnish with a lemon wedge.

*For the chicken stock recipe, refer to page no. 33

This dish is a melange of healthy ingredients and spicy flavours. The coconut milk and lemongrass enhance the taste of the chicken and the noodles. Add to that, the variety of sauces promises a complete South East Asian affair. The distinct aroma is irresistible.

The subtle sweetness of the pumpkin lends a different texture to the chicken. And when cooked in a plethora of aromatic spices, this turns into a winning appetiser.

Roasted Pumpkin and Chicken Soup

Serves: 6

Ingredients

For the Chicken

Chicken 200 gms (boneless & cut into small cubes)
Garlic paste 1 tsp
Ginger paste 1 tsp
Red chilli powder ½ tsp
Cumin (*jeera*) powder ½ tsp
*Garam masala powder ¼ tsp
Salt to taste
Butter 1 tbsp

For the Soup

Olive oil 3 tbsp
Chilli flakes ½ tsp
Cumin (*jeera*) powder 2 tsp
Coriander (*dhania*) powder 1 tsp
Turmeric (*haldi*) powder ½ tsp
Pumpkin 400 gms (peeled & cubed)
Garlic 6 cloves
Onion 1 (sliced)
**Chicken stock 3 cups
Cream 100 ml
Salt to taste
Fresh ground black pepper ½ tsp
Parsley leaves a few (finely chopped to garnish)

Method

- In a bowl, add the chicken cubes and the remaining ingredients except for the butter. Marinate for 20 minutes.
- In another bowl, mix oil, chilli flakes, cumin powder, coriander powder and turmeric powder.
- Add the pumpkin cubes, garlic and onions.
- In a preheated oven, roast the pumpkin mixture at 180˚C for 20 minutes or till the pumpkin is soft and done.
- Allow the pumpkin to cool down and blend into a smooth purée, while adding the chicken stock as required.
- In a saucepan, pour this mixture and bring to a boil. Add cream and season with salt and pepper.
- In another pan, heat the butter and add the marinated cubes of chicken. Fry till the pieces are evenly cooked. Keep aside.
- Place the cooked chicken cubes in the centre of the soup plate, gently pour the soup around.
- Garnish with parsley and serve.

*For the garam masala powder recipe, refer to page no. 8
**For the chicken stock recipe, refer to page no. 33

Gosht Ka Sherwa

Serves: 6

Ingredients

Mutton 400 gms (with bones, preferably neck pieces)
Ginger paste ½ tsp
Garlic paste ½ tsp
Turmeric (*haldi*) powder ½ tsp
Coriander (*dhania*) powder ½ tsp
Onion 1 (sliced)
Tomato 2 (diced)
Black peppercorns 1 tsp
Coriander (*dhania*) leaves 3 tbsp (chopped)
Water 4 cups
Salt to taste

Method

- In a pressure cooker, add the mutton pieces along with all the remaining ingredients and water.
- Cook till the mutton is soft (approximately 8 whistles).
- Turn off the heat and allow the pressure to drop. Open the cooker and keep on simmer for 5 minutes or till the mutton is completely tender. Season with salt.
- Place the mutton pieces in a soup bowl and spoon the hot broth over it.
- Garnish with coriander leaves.

As a child, whenever my mother made this, I'd take a special delight in nibbling on the soft meat and bones of the mutton. This is a fairly easy-to-make recipe that tastes as great as it looks. All you need is some toasted bread slices with butter to relish the dish even better.

I love seafood and this soup is my all-time favourite. With every sip of this delicious broth, there's an explosion of flavours in your mouth.

Spicy Prawn Soup

Serves: 6

Ingredients

Prawns 200 gms (medium size)
Oil 1 tbsp
Lemongrass 2 stalks (1 crushed & the other sliced)
Galangal 3 thin slices
*Chicken stock 4 cups
Kaffir lime leaf 5 (chopped)
Fish sauce 2 tsp
Button mushroom 10 (quartered)
Bird's-eye chilli 2 (very finely chopped)
Lime juice 2 tbsp
Spring onion 2 stalks (green part thinly sliced & put in cold water to get curls)

Method

- Peel and devein the prawns. Leave the tail intact and reserve the heads and shells.
- In a pan, heat the oil.
- Add the prawn heads, shells and cook for 3 minutes until the shells turn bright orange.
- Add one stalk of lemongrass, galangal and chicken stock. Bring to a boil, then reduce the flame and allow to simmer for 15 minutes. Strain the stock.
- Heat the stock and add the remaining lemongrass, Kaffir lime leaves, fish sauce, mushrooms and chillies. Allow to simmer for 10 minutes.
- Add the prawns and cook for 3 minutes or till firm.
- Remove from heat and add the lime juice.
- Garnish with spring onion curls and serve.

*For the Basic Chicken Stock

Ingredients

Chicken 1 kg (without skin)
Water 2½ litres
Carrot 2 (peeled & sliced)
Celery 4 stalks (roughly chopped with leaves)
Onion 2 (peeled & roughly chopped)
Whole black peppercorns 1 tsp
Bay leaf (*tej patta*) 2

Method

- In a pot, put the chicken pieces and add 2½ litres of water and cook over medium-high flame.
- Bring to a boil and then reduce flame to low. Remove the scum (froth).
- Add the carrots, celery, onions, peppercorns and bay leaves.
- Simmer, partially covered, for 1½ hours.
- Place a fine sieve over a large, heatproof bowl. Strain the stock mixture and discard the solids. Set aside to cool. Cover and refrigerate.
- Using a spoon, remove and discard the fat that settles on the surface of the prepared stock.
- Use the stock as required for your soup.

Salads

Fig and Asparagus Salad 37

Couscous Salad with Chickpeas and Red Beans 38

Twice cooked Baby Potato Salad 41

Red Cabbage, Apple and Walnut Salad 42

Mixed Sprouts Salad 45

Roasted Corn, Raw Mango and Peanut Salad 46

Italian Grilled Chicken Salad 48

Zesty Grilled Prawns with Avocado and Mango 51

Oriental Chicken Salad 52

Fresh fig is the show-stopping ingredient here. A very tasty summer salad, this is undoubtedly one of my favourites.

Fig and Asparagus Salad

Serves: 4-5

Ingredients

For the Salad

Asparagus 100 gms	Fresh fig 8 (cut into 4 pieces)
Butter 1 tsp	Pine nuts 2 tbsp (lightly roasted)
Salt to taste	Iceberg lettuce 100 gms (roughly shredded)
Black pepper powder ¼ tsp	Cherry tomato 10 (cut into halves)

For the Dressing

Dry fig 4 (soaked in water overnight)	Red chilli powder ½ tsp
Lemon juice 2 tbsp	Balsamic vinegar ½ tbsp
Honey 2 tsp	Salt to taste
Extra virgin olive oil 2 tbsp	

Method

- Snap the hard ends of the asparagus. In a pan, heat the butter and stir fry the asparagus.
- Season with salt and pepper. Keep aside.
- For the dressing, take a bowl and add the soaked figs. Crush them with your fingers.
- Add the remaining dressing ingredients and mix well.
- In a large mixing bowl, add the asparagus and the remaining salad ingredients. Add the dressing as required.
- Gently toss and serve immediately.

Couscous Salad with Chickpeas and Red Beans

Serves: 4-5

Ingredients

For the Salad

- Couscous 1 cup
- Water 2 cups
- Chickpeas (*kabuli chana*) 1 cup (soaked & boiled)
- Red beans (*rajma*) 1 cup (soaked & boiled)
- Red pepper 1 (finely diced)
- Onion ½ (finely diced)
- Cucumber 2 (deseeded & diced)
- Tomato 1 (finely diced)
- Parsley ½ cup (finely chopped)
- Mint leaves ¼ cup (finely chopped)

For the Dressing

- Olive oil ¼ cup
- Lemon juice extracted out of 1 whole lemon
- Black peppercorns ½ tsp (freshly crushed)
- Cumin (*jeera*) powder ½ tsp
- Salt to taste

Method

- In a bowl, place the couscous and pour 2 cups of boiling water.
- Stir with a fork, cover and set aside for 10 minutes. Once the water is absorbed, fluff up the couscous with a fork to loosen up the grains and keep aside.
- For the dressing, mix olive oil, lemon juice, black pepper, cumin powder and salt in a small jug or bowl.
- In a large mixing bowl, add the couscous with the remaining salad ingredients.
- Stir in the dressing and mix well.
- Serve.

The cumin and mint give this salad a very Middle Eastern flavour. Couscous salad with chickpeas and red beans is best relished with kebabs.

This salad is always a big hit, especially among kids. They can never have enough of baby potatoes. Though slightly higher on the calories, it makes for a great treat once in a while. So, if you want to win your little one's heart, try this recipe at home and experience the joy.

Twice cooked Baby Potato Salad

Serves: 4-5

Ingredients

Baby potatoes 500 gms (washed & parboiled with skin)
Dry flour mixture (3 tbsp all-purpose flour {*maida*}, ½ tsp salt, ½ tsp black pepper powder)
Oil for frying
Eggless mayonnaise 5 tbsp
Tomato ketchup 1 tbsp
Tabasco sauce ½ tbsp
Lemon juice ½ tsp
Oregano ½ tsp
Red chilli powder ½ tsp
Salt to taste
Spring onion 6 stalks (chopped)

Method

- Roll the parboiled baby potatoes in the dry flour mixture.
- In a pan, heat the oil and deep fry the potatoes till crisp. Keep aside to cool down.
- Gently press each potato to flatten them with the help of a spoon.
- In a bowl, mix the mayonnaise, ketchup, Tabasco sauce, lemon juice, oregano, chilli powder and salt.
- In a large bowl, place the potatoes and add the mayonnaise mixture. Mix well and fold the spring onions in.
- Serve.

Red Cabbage, Apple and Walnut Salad

Serves: 4-5

Ingredients

For the Salad

Red cabbage 100 gms (shredded)
White cabbage 100 gms (shredded)
Apple 1 (thinly sliced)
Muscat grapes 10 (cut into half & deseeded)
Walnuts 100 gms
Raisins 50 gms

For the Dressing

Hung curd ½ cup
Eggless mayonnaise 3 tbsp
Cream 50 ml
Lemon juice ½ tbsp
Chilli flakes ½ tsp
Salt to taste

Method

- In a bowl, mix the hung curd, mayonnaise, cream, lemon juice, chilli flakes and salt to make the dressing.
- In a large bowl, add the salad ingredients and mix well.
- Add the dressing and gently toss everything together.
- Serve.

An ideal and a refreshing salad to beat the summer heat, this dish is an explosion of flavours in your mouth. The coleslaw has a light dressing because of the hung curd. Whip up this 'fruity' salad recipe and surprise your loved ones.

This is a simple and super healthy dish. The pomegranate seeds add a crunchy texture to the otherwise mundane sprouts salad. With every spoonful, prepare your palate for a quirky mix of sweet and tangy flavours.

Mixed Sprouts Salad Serves: 4-5

Ingredients

Water as required
Green sprouts (*moong*) 1 cup
Bengal gram sprouts (*kala chana*) 1 cup
Cowpea sprouts (*lobia*) 1 cup
Onion 1 (finely diced)
Tomato 2 (deseeded & finely diced)
Fresh coconut ½ cup (grated)
Green chilli 1 (finely chopped)
Fresh coriander (*dhania*) leaves 2 tbsp (finely chopped)
Lemon juice of 1 whole lemon
Chaat masala ½ tsp
Salt to taste
Pomegranate seeds 1 cup

Method

- In a large pot, boil water and add the sprouts. Parboil, strain and keep aside. Take care not to overcook the sprouts.
- Allow the sprouts to cool down.
- In a bowl, add the sprouts, onions, tomatoes, coconut, green chilli and coriander leaves.
- Mix well.
- Add the lemon juice and chaat masala.
- Season with salt to taste.
- Add the pomegranate seeds and serve.

Roasted Corn, Raw Mango and Peanut Salad

Serves: 4-5

Ingredients

For the Salad

Corn on the cob 2 (husked)	Ripe pineapple 200 gms (cubed)
Raw mango 100 gms (julienned)	Salted peanuts 100 gms

For the Dressing

Green chilli 2	Cumin (*jeera*) seeds ½ tsp
Curry leaves 6	Mango juice 2 tbsp
Mint leaves 8	Lemon juice 1 tbsp
Fresh coriander (*dhania*) leaves (a few)	Jaggery (*gud*) 1 tbsp (grated)
Black peppercorns ¼ tsp	Salt to taste

Method

- Roast the corn on a grill or a stove. Remove the kernels from the cob with a knife.
- For the dressing, crush the green chillies, curry leaves, mint, coriander leaves, peppercorns and cumin seeds into a coarse paste using mortar and pestle.
- In a small bowl, add the mango juice, the previously crushed coarse paste, lemon juice, jaggery and salt. Mix well and keep aside.
- To prepare the salad, add the raw mango, pineapple cubes, roasted corn kernels and peanuts in a mixing bowl.
- Stir in the dressing as required and serve.

Making this dish is nothing less than a trip down memory lane. As a school kid, bhuna bhutta dipped in green chutney was my comfort snack; the indulgence never failed to uplift my mood. The variety of textures including the zesty, yummy raw mangoes paired with the crusty peanuts left my taste buds tingling. This recipe is a must-try!

Italian Grilled Chicken Salad

Serves: 4-5

Ingredients

For the Dressing

English mustard 1 tsp
Garlic 6 cloves
Black pepper powder ½ tsp
Dry oregano ½ tsp
Vinegar 1½ tbsp
Sugar 1 tsp
Olive oil 50 ml
Salt to taste

For the Grilled Chicken

Chicken 200 gms (boneless breast pieces)
Dried Italian herb mix 2 tbsp (oregano, basil, thyme)
Black pepper powder 1 tsp
All-purpose flour (*maida*) 1 tbsp
Salt to taste
Olive oil 2 tbsp

For the Salad

Iceberg lettuce 50 gms (roughly shredded)
Green lettuce 50 gms (roughly shredded)
Pitted black olives 50 gms
Cucumber 1 (sliced)
Tomato 1 (deseeded & diced)
Yellow bell pepper 1 (diced)
Carrot 1 (sliced)

Method

- Combine all the ingredients for the dressing in a blender and whisk vigorously until emulsified.
- Refrigerate the dressing before adding to the salad.
- In a bowl, combine the Italian herb mix, pepper powder, flour and salt. Add the chicken pieces in this mix and coat all sides evenly.
- In a grill pan, heat the olive oil.
- Grill the chicken on both sides till golden brown and done.
- Cover and let the chicken rest and then slice it.
- In a large bowl, combine all the salad ingredients, add the dressing and toss lightly.
- On a serving plate, layer the salad, arrange the sliced chicken on top, drizzle extra dressing over the chicken and serve.

You can easily be deceived because this salad makes for an excellent main course dish too. The aroma from the herb mix in this salad is intoxicating. Giving it a miss wouldn't be a wise decision. So, the next time you play host to a gathering of friends and relatives at home, remember to put this on the menu.

Mangoes and avocados make an irresistible combination. This salad tastes equally delicious when clubbed with chicken or fish.

Zesty Grilled Prawns with Avocado and Mango

Serves: 4-5

Ingredients

For the Marinade

Garlic paste ½ tsp
Black pepper powder ½ tsp
Chilli flakes ½ tsp
Lemon juice 1 tbsp
Lemon zest ½ tsp
Fresh coriander (*dhania*) leaves 1 tbsp, (finely chopped)
Hung curd 2 tbsp
Olive oil 1 tbsp
Salt to taste
Prawns 200 gms (shell removed & deveined; leave the tails intact; wash under running water)
Wooden skewers (a few)

For the Dressing

Lemon juice 1 tbsp
Orange juice 2 tbsp
Castor sugar 1 tbsp
Black pepper powder ½ tsp
Olive oil 3 tbsp
Salt to taste

For the Salad

Avocado 1 (peeled, stoned & flesh cut into cubes)
Ripe mango 2 (peeled & cut into cubes)
Red oak leaf lettuce 100 gms (roughly torn)
Onion 1 (thinly sliced)

Method

- In a bowl, add all the marinade ingredients and mix well.
- Add the prawns. Mix, cover and allow to marinate.
- Thread the marinated prawns on the skewers.
- In a separate bowl, mix the ingredients for the dressing and keep aside.
- Preheat a grill pan and add little oil. Grill the prawns till both sides are done (approximately 2 minutes on each side).
- In a large bowl, combine the salad ingredients, stir in the dressing and toss gently.
- On a serving plate, layer the salad, place the grilled prawn skewers and serve.

Oriental Chicken Salad

Serves: 4-5

Ingredients

For the Marinade

- Garlic paste ½ tsp
- Oyster sauce 2 tbsp
- Black pepper powder ½ tsp
- Salt to taste
- Chicken 250 gms (boneless breast pieces)
- Oil 1 tbsp

For the Dressing

- Ginger ½ tsp (grated)
- Garlic ½ tsp (very finely chopped)
- Fish sauce 1 tbsp
- Lime juice 2 tbsp
- Brown sugar 1 tbsp
- Rice vinegar 1 tbsp
- Fresh red chilli 1 (very finely chopped)

For the Salad

- Rice vermicelli noodles 50 gms
- French beans 100 gms (trimmed & cut into 2-inches length wise, boiled until just tender)
- Cabbage 100 gms (shredded)
- Carrot 1 (julienned)
- Cucumber 1 (julienned)
- Red bell pepper 1 (julienned)
- Fresh coriander (*dhania*) leaves (a few)
- Salted peanuts a few to garnish (roughly chopped)

Method

- Mix all the marinade ingredients except oil.
- Rub the marinade on the chicken breast pieces and allow to marinate for half an hour.
- In a bowl, place the noodles and cover with boiling water. Allow to soak for 5 minutes or until soft. Drain the noodles and keep aside.
- In a pan, heat the oil. Add the marinated chicken breast pieces and fry on both sides till done. Leave it to cool down and cut into cubes.
- Mix all the dressing ingredients together and keep aside.
- In a large bowl, add the chicken cubes, rice noodles and the remaining salad ingredients. Mix well.
- Drizzle the dressing on top and toss gently.
- Garnish with peanuts and serve.

When melt-in-your-mouth chicken cubes team up with crunchy vegetables and noodles, the result is a salad to die for! A platter of this salad is as good a wholesome meal to relish for lunch or dinner.

Vegetarian

This can be served as both a salad and a starter, and is full of fresh flavours. To enjoy it best, use fresh mozzarella cheese.

Pesto Zucchini Cups

Serves: Makes 15 cups

Ingredients

For the Zucchini Cups

Green zucchini 2
Olive oil 2 tbsp
Salt to taste
Black pepper powder ½ tsp

For the Pesto

Fresh basil (*tulsi*) leaves 1 cup
Pine nuts 3 tbsp (if not available, you can use 10 cashew nuts)
Balsamic vinegar ½ tbsp
Parmesan cheese 2 tbsp (grated)
Garlic 4 cloves
Olive oil ¼ cup
Salt to taste
Fresh mozzarella cheese 100 gms (cut into small cubes)
Cherry tomato 10 (quartered)

Method

- Preheat the oven to 180° C. Peel the zucchini leaving some strips intact.
- Cut the zucchini into 2.5-inch thick slices.
- In a mixing bowl, combine the zucchini with olive oil, salt and black pepper powder. Keep aside for 10 minutes.
- For the Pesto, add the basil leaves, pine nuts or cashew nuts, balsamic vinegar, Parmesan and garlic in a blender. Keep adding the olive oil, bit by bit, till it is well incorporated and the paste turns smooth.
- Season with salt to taste.
- Store in an airtight container, refrigerate and use as required.
- In a mixing bowl, combine the mozzarella cheese and cherry tomatoes with 2 tablespoons of the prepared Pesto and keep aside.
- On a greased baking tray, arrange the marinated zucchini and grill in the preheated oven for about 12 minutes.
- When done, remove from oven and allow it to cool down. Scoop out a bit from the centre to form small cups.
- Fill these cups with the cheese and cherry tomato mixture.
- Arrange the filled cups on a serving platter.
- Garnish with a few basil leaves. Serve immediately.

This is a Middle Eastern recipe. While most of the ingredients listed here can be found in any Indian home, I suggest you use only good quality olive oil to make the hummus tastier. If parsley is not readily available, you can choose coriander as the next best substitute. Let me guarantee you that when you serve this rendition of falafel with hummus to your guests, they will instantly fall in love with this dish.

Falafel with Hummus

Serves: 4-5

Ingredients

For the Falafel

- Dry chickpeas (*kabuli chana*) 1½ cups, (soaked overnight)
- Parsley ¾ cup (finely chopped)
- Fresh coriander (*dhania*) leaves ½ cup, (finely chopped)
- Onion 2 (finely diced)
- Garlic 2 tbsp (finely chopped)
- Coriander (*dhania*) powder 2 tsp
- Cumin (*jeera*) powder 1 tsp
- Red chilli powder 2 tsp
- Salt to taste
- Oil for deep frying

For the Hummus

- Dry chickpeas (*kabuli chana*) ½ cup (soaked overnight & boiled)
- Garlic 1 tsp (finely chopped)
- Extra virgin olive oil ½ cup
- Lemon juice 1½ tbsp
- *Tahini paste 2 tbsp
- Salt to taste
- Cucumber sticks, pita bread, olives to serve

Method

- For the falafel, put the soaked chickpeas in a blender and pulse to make a coarse paste.
- Add this to a bowl and mix with parsley (if not available, use coriander leaves in greater quantity), coriander leaves, onion, garlic, coriander powder, cumin powder, red chilli powder and salt.
- Mix well and divide into small portions. Shape each portion into a small ball and slightly flatten it in the centre.
- In a deep pan or kadai, heat the oil and deep fry the falafel till golden and crisp.
- For the hummus, add the boiled chickpeas in a blender.
- Add the garlic, olive oil, lemon juice, tahini and salt. (Remember to add the olive oil in batches.)
- Blend till the mixture is creamy and smooth.
- Remove in a serving bowl and drizzle some olive oil. Sprinkle a pinch of red chilli powder.
- To serve, arrange the falafel, cucumber sticks, pita bread, olives and hummus on a platter.

* For the Tahini paste, grind 1 cup of sesame seeds along with ½ cup of olive oil into a smooth paste. Refrigerate and use as required.

Paneer and Pineapple Skewers

Serves: 4-5

Ingredients

Cottage cheese (*paneer*) 200 gms
Ripe pineapple 200 gms
Onion 1
Red bell pepper 1
Yellow bell pepper 1

For the Marinade

Garlic paste 1 tsp
Red chilli powder ½ tsp
Cumin (*jeera*) powder 1 tsp
Dark soya sauce 2 tbsp
Tomato ketchup 6 tbsp
Black pepper powder ½ tsp
Sugar 1 tsp
Salt to taste
Oil 3 tbsp

Method

- Cut the paneer and pineapple into cubes of the same size.
- Dice the onion and peppers.
- In a bowl, mix all the ingredients to prepare the marinade. Add the paneer, pineapple cubes and diced vegetables.
- Thread the marinated paneer, pineapple and vegetables and arrange them on the skewers alternately.
- In a grill pan, heat the oil and fry the skewers.
- Serve hot.

This is a quick and easy-to-make dish. It works as a great option during cocktail parties or when unexpected guests decide to land up for dinner.

This Burmese noodle dish is my all-time favourite. It's actually a one-pot meal. With the toppings suggested here, this mouth-watering delicacy can work wonders during house parties and get-togethers.

Khow Suey

Serves: 4-5

Ingredients

Onion 2 (diced)
Ginger 1-inch piece
Garlic 12 cloves
Lemongrass 2 stalks (crushed)
Oil 4 tbsp
Turmeric (*haldi*) powder ½ tsp
Coriander (*dhania*) powder 1 tsp
Red chilli powder 1 tsp
Chilli flakes 1 tsp
Chopped vegetables 400 gms, (carrots, French beans, baby corn, broccoli, mushrooms, red bell pepper, yellow zucchini, green zucchini)
*Vegetable stock 2 cups (you can also prepare stock by diluting 1 vegetable stock cube / bouillon with 2 cups of hot water)
Gram flour (*besan*) 2 tbsp
Water ½ cup
Coconut milk 200 ml
Brown sugar 1 tsp
Soya sauce 1 tsp
Salt to taste
Boiled noodles 200 gms

For the Topping

Fried noodles 100 gms (deep fry the boiled noodles till golden brown)
Roasted peanuts ¼ cup
Spring onions ¼ cup (sliced)
Fried onions ¼ cup
Fresh coriander (*dhania*) leaves ¼ cup (finely chopped)
**Chilli oil 2 tbsp

Method

- Blend the onions, ginger, garlic and lemongrass into a smooth paste.
- In a pan, heat the oil and add the paste. Gently sauté for about 3 minutes.
- Add the turmeric powder, coriander powder, chilli powder, chilli flakes and sauté for another minute. Add the chopped vegetables and sauté for a minute. Add the stock and cook till the vegetables are tender but crisp.
- In a small pan, on low flame, dry roast the gram flour until the raw smell has completely gone away. Keep aside to cool down. Mix well in half a cup of water. Make sure there are no lumps formed while mixing.
- Slowly, stir the gram flour mixture into the vegetable broth and cook till the broth slightly thickens.
- Add the coconut milk, brown sugar, soya sauce and salt. Stir and remove from heat.
- To serve, place the boiled noodles in a deep bowl, then add enough hot broth to cover the noodles. Place the fried noodles on top and serve with the various toppings.

*For the vegetable stock recipe, refer to page no. 18

**For the chilli oil recipe, refer to page no. 9

Stuffed Aubergine Rolls

Serves: 4-5

Ingredients

Aubergine / Eggplant 2
Black pepper powder ½ tsp
Salt to taste
Olive oil 2 tbsp

For the Filling

Cream cheese 200 gms
Onion 1 (finely diced)
Tomato 1 (deseeded & finely diced)
Fresh coriander (*dhania*) leaves 2 tbsp (finely chopped)
Fresh parsley 2 tbsp (finely chopped)
Walnuts ¼ cup (roughly chopped)
Garlic 1 tsp (finely chopped)
Black pepper powder ½ tsp
Lemon juice 1 tbsp
Salt to taste

Method

- Cut the eggplant lengthwise into thin slices, sprinkle salt and pepper on both sides.
- In a grill pan, heat the olive oil and grill the eggplant slices for 3 minutes on both sides and keep aside.
- In a bowl, mix all the ingredients for the filling.
- Put 1 tablespoon of the filling mixture on one end of the eggplant slice. Gently roll it.
- Repeat with all the remaining slices. Place the eggplant rolls on a serving plate and garnish with chopped parsley. Serve.

For most kids, brinjal is the monster veggie. But these eggplant rolls have a creamy cheese filling combined with the extra crunch of crushed walnuts that will certainly make a hero out of the 'monster' veggie. Serve these delicious rolls to your kids and watch them crave for more helpings.

Our good old upma is back in an all-new avatar. The mushroom topping gives this classic dish a wonderful twist, making this a great breakfast option.

Grilled Semolina with Mushroom Topping

Serves: 4-5

Ingredients

Semolina (*sooji*) ½ cup
Milk 1 cup
Water ½ cup
Butter 2 tbsp
Cheese 2 slices
Black pepper powder ½ tsp
Dry oregano ½ tsp
Salt to taste

For the Mushroom Topping

Olive oil 2 tbsp
Onion 1 (finely diced)
Garlic 1 tsp (finely chopped)
Button mushroom 250 gms (finely diced)
Salt to taste
Black pepper powder ½ tsp
Balsamic vinegar ½ tbsp
Cream 5 tbsp
Fresh thyme leaves 1 tsp (chopped)
Fresh parsley 2 tbsp (finely chopped)
Oil 1 tbsp (for grilling)

Method

- Heat a non-stick pan and on low flame, dry roast the semolina. Keep aside to cool down completely before using.
- In a saucepan, heat the milk and water. Add butter, cheese slices, pepper, oregano and salt.
- Once the mixture starts boiling, reduce heat and gradually add the roasted semolina, stirring continuously to prevent lumps. Cover, reduce the flame and cook for 3 minutes.
- Remove the pan from the stove. Line/grease a baking tray with oil.
- Spread the cooked semolina mixture evenly with a spatula. Keep aside. Refrigerate.
- In a pan, heat the olive oil. Add the onions and sauté till translucent. Add the garlic and fry for a minute.
- Add the mushrooms and sauté until most of the moisture has evaporated.
- Season with salt and pepper to taste.
- Add the balsamic vinegar, cream and thyme and cook for a minute. Turn off the heat and add the parsley. Mix well.
- Cut the set semolina into squares.
- In a grill pan, heat the oil and grill the squares on both sides. Spoon the mushroom mixture on each of the grilled semolina square. Serve.

Pumpkin and Peanut Subzi with Akki Roti

Serves: 4-5

Ingredients

Oil ¼ cup	Coriander (*dhania*) powder 1 tsp
Onion 2 (finely diced)	Turmeric (*haldi*) powder ½ tsp
Ginger paste 1 tsp	Fresh coriander (*dhania*) leaves 3 tbsp (chopped)
Garlic paste 1 tsp	Pumpkin 600 gms (peeled & cubed)
Tomato 2 (finely diced)	Salt to taste
Red chilli powder 1 tsp	

For the Peanut Masala

Peanuts 100 gms (dry roasted & skin removed)	Garlic 10 cloves
Long, dry red chilli (*Kashmiri*) 8 (dry roasted)	

Method

- In a pan, heat the oil. Add the onions and fry till golden brown.
- Add the ginger-garlic pastes and fry for a minute.
- Add the tomatoes, chilli powder, coriander powder, turmeric powder, coriander leaves and fry till the tomatoes become soft.
- Add the pumpkin cubes and sauté. Add salt and cook till the pumpkin is soft and done.
- Coarsely grind the peanut masala ingredients and add to the cooked pumpkin.
- Garnish with coriander leaves and serve with hot akki rotis and ghee.

For the Akki Roti

Water 2½ cups	Rice flour 2 cups
Salt to taste	

Method

- Boil the water with salt. Take the rice flour in a wide bowl and add the hot water slowly.
- Mix with the help of a spoon and keep aside.
- Let the mixture cool down so that you can start kneading the dough.

- Gently mix and knead into a soft dough. Ensure that the dough does not crack or turn crumbly; if it is very dry or too thin or soft, you would find it difficult to roll. Divide the dough into small balls.
- Place one dough ball on a working surface, dust with rice flour and flatten with your palms and fingers. Press and spread evenly and as thinly as possible, or use a rolling pin and gently roll into a roti.
- Gently transfer the roti on to the preheated tawa. Cook on medium flame.
- Once you see bubbles forming on the roti, flip it and cook the other side. Roll the remaining rotis, and repeat the cooking process.

The combination of pumpkin and peanuts works brilliantly in this typical breakfast recipe. Akki roti is a popular dish in Karnataka—essentially rice bread—and requires a lot of practice to get it right. Don't forget to drizzle some ghee before serving.

A very popular vegetarian dish from Karnataka, bisi means ‘hot’, belle ‘lentils’ and bhath is ‘rice’. I learnt this recipe from my mother-in-law. A ready-to-mix masala is easily available in stores, but a homemade masala is always better. I personally enjoy this with potato wafers.

Bisi Belle Bhath

Serves: 4-5

Ingredients

Water 4 cups
Pigeon peas (*toor dal / arhar dal*) 1 cup
Oil 2 tbsp
Rice 1½ cups
Mixed diced vegetables 300 gms (carrot, French beans, knol khol—also known as kohlrabi, similar to turnip {optional}— & green peas)
Tamarind (*imli*) 70 gms (soaked in 1 cup of warm water for 15 minutes, squeezed & pulp extracted)
Jaggery (*gud*) 1 tbsp (grated)
Dry coconut ½ cup (grated & dry roasted)
Salt to taste
Potato wafers, raita, to serve

For the Spice Powder

Oil 3 tbsp (for roasting the spices)
Long, dry red chillies (*Kashmiri*) ¾ cup
Coriander (*dhania*) seeds ½ cup
Kopak buds (*Marathi moggu*) 5
Cinnamon (*dalchini*) 2 sticks
Cardamom (*elaichi*) 2 pods
Clove (*laung*) 8

For the Tempering

Clarified butter (*ghee*) 2 tbsp
Oil 1 tbsp
Mustard (*rai*) seeds ½ tsp
Long, dry red chilli (*Kashmiri*) 2 (broken in half)
Curry leaves 15
Cashew nuts 75 gms
Asafoetida (*hing*) ¼ tsp

Method

- In a pan, heat the oil and roast all the spices on low flame.
- Allow them to cool down and grind into a powder.
- In a deep pot, boil the water and add the washed dal with 2 tablespoons of oil.
- Cook till the dal is half done and then add the washed rice.
- Cook till the dal is completely done and the rice is soft.
- Add the chopped vegetables and cook until they are tender.
- In a separate pan, heat the tamarind pulp, add the prepared spice powder, jaggery and roasted coconut, and bring to a boil. Add this to the cooked dal and rice mixture. Season with salt.
- Simmer and cook for 15 minutes till everything is well mixed. Add more water if required.
- To prepare the tempering, in a separate pan, heat the ghee and oil. Add the mustard seeds, and once they crackle, add the remaining ingredients. Fry till the cashew nuts turn golden brown.
- Pour the tempering on the prepared Bisi Belle Bhath. Cover and allow the flavours to infuse in the rice. Serve hot with raita or potato wafers.

Haryali Burger

Serves: 4-5

Ingredients

Butter 2 tbsp
Onion 1 (finely diced)
Green chilli 2 (finely chopped)
Ginger paste 1 tsp
Garlic paste 1 tsp
Broccoli florets 200 gms (grated along with stem)
Spinach leaves 250 gms (chopped)
Green peas 200 gms (boiled & mashed)
Black pepper powder 1 tsp
Mango powder (*aamchoor*) ¼ tsp
*Garam masala powder ½ tsp
Potato 2 (peeled, boiled & grated)
Fresh coriander (*dhania*) leaves 3 tbsp (chopped)
Fresh paneer 100 gms (grated)
Bread 4 slices (dried, roughly chopped & blended in a mixer to make crumbs)
Salt to taste
Oats 3 tbsp
Mint chutney 3 tsp
Mayonnaise 5 tbsp
Burger bun 5
Tomato ketchup 5 tbsp
Lettuce leaves 5-6
Cheese 5 slices
Oil 4 tbsp (for frying)

Method

- In a pan, heat the butter. Add the onion and fry till translucent.
- Add the green chillies, ginger-garlic pastes. Sauté for a minute.
- Add the broccoli, spinach leaves, peas and sauté for 3 minutes.
- Remove the pan from heat and add the dry masalas, grated potatoes, coriander, paneer, breadcrumbs and salt. Mix well.
- Divide the mixture into equal portions and shape them into patties (make them the same size as the burger buns).
- Roll the patties in oats and shallow fry them till golden brown on both sides.
- In a small bowl, mix the mint chutney and mayonnaise.
- Slice the burger buns into halves, apply butter and toast them.
- Spread the mint-mayonnaise chutney on the lower half and ketchup on the upper half.
- Place the lettuce at the base. Next, place the patty on top of the lettuce.
- Top each patty with a cheese slice; close the burger with the other half.
- Press lightly and serve immediately with wafers.

*For the garam masala powder recipe, refer to page no. 8

Packed with nutrition, this haryali burger is a healthy and filling snack option. It is a clever way to make children eat vegetables they might otherwise detest.

Every time I make them, my friends suspect if the kebabs are really vegetarian! Rajma and methi kebabs is the veggie version of shammi kebabs, or so I'd like to call them.

Rajma and Methi Kebabs

Serves: Makes 15-20 kebabs

Ingredients

Oil 2 tbsp + for frying
Onion 1 (finely chopped)
Ginger paste 1 tsp
Garlic paste 1 tsp
Tomato 1 (finely chopped)
Chilli flakes ½ tsp
Cumin (*jeera*) powder 1 tsp
Red chilli powder 1 tsp
Black pepper powder 1 tsp
*Garam masala powder ½ tsp
Fresh coconut ¼ cup (grated)
Fresh fenugreek (*methi*) leaves 1 cup
Dry kidney beans (*rajma*) 200 gms (soaked overnight & boiled)
Salt to taste
All-purpose flour (*maida*) ¼ cup
Water as required
Breadcrumbs 1 cup

For the Methi Cream Sauce

Fresh cream 200 ml
Cheese 4 slices
Black pepper powder ½ tsp
Dry fenugreek (*kasoori methi*) leaves 1 tsp
Salt to taste

Method

- In a pan, heat 2 tablespoons of oil, add chopped onions and fry for a minute.
- Add the ginger-garlic pastes, sauté till the onions are translucent.
- Add the tomato, chilli flakes, cumin powder, red chilli powder, black pepper powder, garam masala powder and sauté till the tomatoes become soft.
- Add the grated coconut and sauté for half a minute.
- Add the fenugreek leaves and fry for a minute. Add the boiled rajma, salt and mix well.
- Cook till the mixture turns dry, remove from flame. Keep aside and allow it to cool down.
- Grind the mixture into a smooth paste. Divide this mixture into small, round balls and give them an oblong shape.
- Make a thin slurry (or paste) with flour and water.
- Dip the kebabs in the slurry and roll on the breadcrumbs till well-coated. Keep aside.
- In a separate pan, boil the cream, add cheese slices, black pepper powder, dry fenugreek, salt and stir. Cook till the cheese melts and the sauce slightly thickens. Remove from flame and keep aside.
- In a pan, heat the oil and deep fry the kebabs till golden brown. Serve hot with the sauce.

*For the garam masala powder recipe, refer to page no. 8

Crispy Vegetables with Tomato Chutney

Serves: 6-8

Ingredients

Ridge gourd (*turai*) 100 gms (peeled, cut into ½-inch slices & core removed)
Cauliflower florets 100 gms
Broccoli florets 100 gms
Baby corn 100 gms (diagonally sliced)
Onion 1 (cut into rings)
Oil for frying
Chaat masala to garnish

For the Dry Coating

Cornstarch ¼ cup
Red chilli powder 1 tsp
Salt to taste

For the Batter

Cornstarch ½ cup
All-purpose flour (*maida*) ½ cup
Baking powder ½ tsp
*Garam masala powder ½ tsp
Red chilli powder 1 tsp
Chilled club soda as required
Salt to taste
Oil for frying

Method

- In a bowl, mix all the ingredients together for the dry coating.
- Add the vegetables and mix well till everything is coated evenly.
- In a deep pan or kadai, heat the oil.
- In a separate mixing bowl, whisk all the batter ingredients together.
- Add the chilled soda (as required) and mix to make a smooth batter (the batter should be thick enough to coat the vegetables) without any lumps.
- Dip the vegetables in the batter and fry till golden brown. Fry all the vegetables in batches.
- Sprinkle chaat masala and serve with tomato chutney.

For the Tomato Chutney

Water 2 cups
Tomato 4
Long, dry red chilli (*Kashmiri*) 8
Tamarind (*imli*) (a small lemon-sized ball)
Onion ½ (sliced)
Garlic 20 cloves (with skin) + 4 cloves (crushed)
Cumin (*jeera*) seeds 1 tsp
Fenugreek (*methi*) seeds ¼ tsp
Oil 4 tbsp
Mustard (*rai*) seeds ½ tsp
Curry leaves 15
Sugar 2 tsp
Salt to taste

Method

- In a deep pot, add water, tomatoes, dry chillies, tamarind, onion and garlic (with skin).
- Boil till the tomatoes are soft. Allow the mixture to cool down and blend into a smooth purée.
- Strain the purée and keep aside.
- Dry roast the cumin and fenugreek seeds, and crush into a coarse powder.
- In a pan, heat the oil and add the mustard seeds. When they begin to splutter, add the crushed garlic and fry till golden brown.
- Add the curry leaves, prepared cumin and fenugreek powder. Sauté for half a minute.
- Add the tomato purée, sugar and cook on medium flame till you get a thick sauce-like consistency and the oil separates. Season with salt.

*For the garam masala powder recipe, refer to page no. 8

The batter here is deliciously crisp, light and golden in colour. It can be relished with tomato ketchup as well but I'd recommend you to pick the tomato chutney I've included in this recipe. Let me promise you, the taste shall be enhanced by a few notches. You are free to use any vegetable(s) of your choice.

Potato Dumplings

Serves: Makes 25 dumplings

Ingredients

For the Dough

All-purpose flour (*maida*) 1½ cups
Salt ¼ tsp
Water as required
Oil 1 tsp
Cornstarch 2 tbsp (for dusting)

For the Filling

Potato 2 (boiled & grated)
Spring onions ½ cup (white part finely chopped) + ½ cup (green part finely chopped)
Green chilli 2 (very finely chopped)
Black pepper powder ½ tsp
Butter 50 gms (room temperature)
Salt to taste
Bok Choy or lettuce leaves for steaming

Method

- In a large bowl, mix the ingredients for the dough and knead to form a stiff but soft dough.
- Cover and keep aside.
- Mix all the ingredients, for the filling, in a bowl, till well combined.
- Divide the dough into small balls.
- Roll into small 4- to 5-inch circles (use cornstarch for dusting).
- Choose a circle, wet the edges and place some filling in the centre.
- Bring the edges together to cover the filling, twist to seal or just simply fold the other half and press the edges. Repeat to prepare more dumplings.
- In a steamer or rice cooker, heat the water.
- Line the basket with Bok Choy or lettuce leaves. Place the dumplings (space them out so that they do not stick).
- Place the basket on the steamer when the water starts boiling and steam for 5 to 7 minutes.
- Garnish with spring onions. Serve with chilli sauce.

For the Chilli Sauce

Oil 2 tbsp
Ginger paste 1 tsp
Garlic paste 1 tsp
Chilli flakes 1 tbsp
Vinegar 5 tbsp
Brown sugar 2 tbsp
Salt to taste
Tomato purée 2 tbsp
Tomato sauce 4 tbsp

Method

- In a pan, heat the oil and add the ginger-garlic pastes and fry for a minute.
- Reduce the heat and add the chilli flakes. Fry for half a minute.
- Add the vinegar, brown sugar, salt, tomato purée, tomato sauce and bring the sauce to boil, till thick.
- Serve the dumplings with this chilli sauce.

This is a dish that refreshes my childhood memories of visiting Kerala with my grandfather. I loved this stew, and I especially enjoyed relishing it with my family. It is simple, yet bursting with flavours. My tip to you would be: prepare the stew with freshly extracted coconut milk. My twist to the humble vegetable stew is the paneer cubes. Bon appétit!

Vegetable Stew

Serves: 4

Ingredients

Oil 2 tbsp
Mustard (*rai*) seeds ½ tsp
Curry leaves 10
Onion 1 (finely diced)
Ginger paste ½ tsp
Garlic paste ½ tsp
Green chilli 1 (finely chopped)
Mixed vegetables cut into small cubes 250 gms, (potato, French beans, peas, baby corn, carrot)
Black peppercorns ½ tsp (crushed)
Fresh paneer 50 gms (diced)
*Fresh coconut milk 1½ cups (thin in consistency) + 1 cup (thick in consistency)
Spice mix (4 cloves, 3 cardamom pods, 1 cinnamon stick, ½ tsp pepper, ½ tsp fennel {*saunf*} seeds tied in a muslin cloth)
Salt to taste
String hoppers / idiyappams to serve

Method

- In a pan, heat the oil and add the mustard seeds.
- Once they begin to splutter, add the curry leaves, onion, ginger-garlic pastes, green chilli and fry till the onions are translucent. (Be careful not to brown the onions).
- Add the mixed vegetables and sauté for a minute.
- Add the crushed black pepper.
- Reduce heat, cover and cook the vegetables till half done.
- Add the paneer cubes and cook for a minute.
- Add the thin coconut milk, the spices which have been tied in the muslin cloth and salt.
- Cook on medium flame till the flavour of the spices has been infused and the vegetables are fully done.
- Add the thick coconut milk and bring the stew to boil.
- Before serving the stew, remove the spices which have been tied in a muslin cloth.
- Serve with string hoppers or idiyappams.

*For the fresh coconut milk recipe, refer to page no. 9

Chicken

Chicken and Cheese Balls with Tomato Basil Sauce 85

Lebanese Chicken Skewers 86

Thai Green Curry with Steamed Coconut Rice 88

Methi Murg (creamy Fenugreek Chicken) 90

Tandoori Chicken and Spinach Roulade 92

Chicken Masala Crêpe Parcels 95

Murg Makai Kebabs (corn and Chicken Kebabs) 96

Fried Chicken Kebabs 99

Hunan Chicken with Rice and Noodles 100

Murg Haleem 102

Kachee Murg Biryani 105

Dum Ki Murg 108

Cheesy Nachos with Chicken Keema 110

Pepper Chicken Steak with Creamy Mashed Potatoes 112

Grilled Chicken with Mexican Rice 114

Here is a quick and easy teatime snack recipe. These crispy chicken balls filled with cheese work wonders as an appetiser. The tangy flavour of the tomato basil sauce lends this finger-licking dish a unique taste.

Chicken and Cheese Balls with Tomato Basil Sauce

Serves: Makes 15

Ingredients

For the Filling

Oil 2 tbsp + for frying	Water ½ cup
Garlic paste 1 tbsp	Green chilli 5 (finely chopped)
Chicken 500 gms (medium size pieces with bones)	Fresh coriander (*dhania*) leaves 4 tbsp (finely chopped)
Black pepper powder 1½ tsp	Mozzarella cheese 100 gms (grated)
Cumin (*jeera*) powder 1½ tsp	Cheddar cheese 100 gms (grated)
Salt to taste	Bread 15 slices

Method

- In a pan, heat 2 tablespoons of oil. Add the garlic paste and fry for half a minute.
- Add the chicken pieces and fry for 3 minutes. Add pepper powder, cumin powder and salt.
- Add the water, cover and cook on medium flame till the chicken is done and the masala has coated the chicken evenly. Keep aside to cool down. Shred the pieces.
- In a large bowl, add the shredded chicken, green chillies, coriander and grated cheese and mix well. Make egg-sized balls from this mixture.
- Cut the sides from the bread slices. Take some water in a bowl, dip each bread slice slightly and gently press them between your palms to squeeze out the excess water. Be careful not to soak the bread completely; it should be moist enough to wrap the chicken.
- Place the previously prepared chicken balls in the centre of each bread slice, press and cover from all sides. In a deep pan/kadai, heat the oil. Fry the chicken balls till golden brown.
- Serve with tomato basil sauce.

For the Tomato Basil Sauce

Oil 2 tbsp	Black pepper powder ½ tsp
Garlic 1 tbsp (finely chopped)	Sugar 1 tsp
Tomato purée 1 cup	Salt to taste
Tomatoes ½ cup (chopped)	Basil (*tulsi*) leaves 8 (chopped)

Method

- In a pan, heat the oil. Add the garlic and fry till golden brown.
- Add the tomato purée and chopped tomatoes; sauté for 2 minutes till soft.
- Add the pepper powder, sugar and salt. Cook for another minute.
- Remove from flame and add the basil leaves.

Lebanese Chicken Skewers

Serves: Makes 15 skewers

Ingredients

Chicken 600 gms (boneless thigh pieces cut into cubes)
Bamboo skewers 15
Oil 2 tbsp (for frying)

For the Marinade

Hung curd 2 tbsp
Long, dry red chilli (*Kashmiri*) 4 (boiled & kept aside)
Ginger paste 1 tsp
Garlic paste 1 tsp
Tomato paste 1 tbsp
Lemon juice extracted out of 1 whole lemon
*Spice mix 1 tsp
Olive oil 1 tbsp
Salt to taste

Method

- In a mixer, blend the hung curd and chillies together.
- Remove in a bowl and add all the remaining marinade ingredients.
- Add the chicken pieces, cover and refrigerate for 4-5 hours.
- Thread the marinated chicken pieces on the skewers.
- In a grill pan, heat 2 tablespoons of oil.
- Fry the chicken on both sides, till done.
- Serve hot with yoghurt-garlic dip.

For the Yoghurt-Garlic Dip

Hung curd ½ cup
Mayonnaise 3 tbsp
Garlic paste ½ tsp
Lemon juice ½ tsp
Salt to taste

Method

- Whisk all the ingredients in a bowl until smooth and well combined.

*For the Spice Mix

Black pepper powder 2 tbsp
Chilli flakes 2 tbsp
Cumin (*jeera*) seeds 2 tbsp
Coriander (*dhania*) seeds 1 tbsp
Cardamom (*elaichi*) 1 tbsp
Cloves (*laung*) 1 tbsp
Cinnamon (*dalchini*) 4-5 sticks
Allspice (*kabab cheeni*) 7 pods
Nutmeg (*jaiphal*) ½ (grated)

Method

- Dry roast all the ingredients. Keep aside to cool down.
- Blend into a fine powder and store in an airtight container. Use as required.

This is also known as Shish Tawook. Not a complex dish to make, Lebanese chicken skewers is a party winner. Marinating the chicken in a blend of aromatic spices is what makes it an instant hit among foodies. I'd advise you to keep the prepared spice mix powder handy.

Thai Green Curry with Steamed Coconut Rice

Serves: 6-8

Ingredients

For the Paste

Coriander (*dhania*) seeds 1 tsp
Cumin (*jeera*) seeds 1 tsp
Green chilli 15
Lemongrass 2 stalks (only white part, chopped)
Galangal 1-inch piece (chopped)
Kaffir lime leaves 7
Garlic 10 cloves
Asian shallots (*chhote pyaaz)* 5
Fresh coriander (*dhania*) leaves 20 gms (chopped along with the roots)
Thai basil leaves 15
Oil as required

For the Green Curry

Coconut cream 100 ml
Chicken 400 gms (boneless breast pieces, cut into thin strips)
Coconut milk 400 ml
Fish sauce 2 tbsp
Jaggery (*gud)* 1 tbsp
Salt to taste
Galangal 1-inch piece (julienned)
Kaffir lime leaves 5 (roughly shredded)
Fresh red chilli 1 (thinly sliced)
Thai basil leaves (a few to garnish)

Method

- In a pan, dry roast the coriander and cumin seeds.
- Blend all the ingredients for the paste, adding oil as required to assist in blending.
- In a pan, heat the coconut cream on medium flame till the cream separates and a layer of oil forms on the surface.
- Add the paste and sauté until fragrant. Add the chicken and stir for 3 minutes.
- Add the coconut milk, fish sauce, jaggery, salt and cook for 6-8 minutes until the chicken is done. Add the galangal and kaffir lime leaves.
- Garnish with fresh red chilli slices and basil leaves. Serve with steamed coconut rice.

For the Steamed Coconut Rice

Water 3 cups
Ginger 1-inch piece (sliced)
Long grain/Basmati rice 2 cups (washed & soaked for 20 minutes)
Coconut milk 1 cup
Salt to taste

Method

- In a large, deep pot, add the water and ginger and bring to a boil.
- Add the soaked rice, coconut milk and salt. Boil till almost all the liquid has evaporated.
- Cover the pot, reduce the heat and cook the rice till done. (Note: This will take about 8-10 minutes.) Serve the coconut rice with the prepared Thai green curry.

This dish is right up my alley for its bold and beautiful balance of flavours. It is sweet and spicy, salty and sour. Dressing up a plate with the vibrant green Thai curry, alongside the very fragrant coconut rice is my favourite part of the recipe. The play of textures adds a tropical element to the meal. You can prepare more of the curry paste and stock it in the fridge for later use.

Methi Murg (Creamy Fenugreek Chicken)

Serves: 6-8

Ingredients

Chicken 1 kg (medium size pieces with bones)
Curd / yoghurt (*dahi*) 400 gms
White pepper powder ½ tbsp
Dry fenugreek (*kasoori methi*) leaves 3 tbsp
Salt to taste
Oil 3 tbsp
Cream 200 ml

For the Paste

Ginger paste 1 tbsp
Garlic paste 1 tbsp
*Garam masala powder ½ tsp
Green chilli 8
Onion 2 (sliced)

Method

- Marinate the chicken with yoghurt, white pepper powder, dry fenugreek and salt.
- Grind all the ingredients, for the paste, into a smooth consistency.
- In a pan, heat the oil and fry the paste until it changes colour. Add the marinated chicken and reduce the flame.
- Cook for 5 minutes and add a little water.
- Cover and cook the chicken on medium flame until tender.
- Add the cream and cook for another 2 minutes.
- Serve with rice or paranthas.

*For the garam masala powder recipe, refer to page no. 8

This is one of the easiest chicken gravies to prepare. The faint sourness of the yoghurt infuses seamlessly into the chicken. Once the spices seep in, the chicken becomes succulent. The cream lends a special richness to the juicy chicken pieces, making this an ideal dish to be savoured with paranthas or rice.

Tandoori Chicken and Spinach Roulade

Serves: 6

Ingredients

Chicken 400 gms (boneless breast pieces sliced horizontally into half and flattened slightly with a meat mallet or rolling pin)

For the Marinade

Garlic paste 1 tsp
Red chilli powder 2 tsp
Black pepper powder 1 tsp
Cumin (*jeera*) powder 1 tsp
*Garam masala powder ½ tsp
Dry fenugreek (*kasoori methi*) powder 1 tsp
Lemon juice 3 tbsp
Oil 1 tbsp
Salt to taste

For the Filling

Spinach leaves 500 gms (blanched, excess water squeezed out & chopped)
Garlic 1 tsp (finely chopped)
Green chilli 3 (very finely chopped)
*Garam masala powder ¼ tsp
Cheddar cheese 100 gms (grated)
Salt to taste

For the Tzatziki Dip

Cucumber ½ (deseeded & finely chopped)
Garlic 1 tbsp (finely chopped)
Hung curd 1 cup
Olive oil 1 tbsp
Lemon juice 1 tbsp
Mint leaves 2 tbsp (finely chopped)
Black pepper powder ½ tsp
Salt to taste

Method

- In a bowl, mix all the marinade ingredients.
- Spread the masala evenly on the chicken slices and marinate for an hour.
- In a large bowl, mix all the ingredients for the filling.
- Place the flattened chicken pieces on a board. Spoon the filling on it and carefully roll up the chicken to form a roulade. Secure the end of the chicken roll with a toothpick.
- Repeat the process with all the other chicken slices.
- Place the roulades on a baking tray.
- Grill in a preheated oven at 220°C for 15 minutes, till the chicken is done and turns golden brown.
- Smear some butter on top of the roulades. Remove the toothpick. Cut the roulades diagonally into halves.
- In a bowl, mix all the ingredients for the Tzatziki dip and serve with roulades.

*For the garam masala powder recipe, refer to page no. 8

Isn't tandoori chicken just about everyone's favourite? I have attempted a twist to the classic dish with this recipe. Roulade means 'rolled meat' or 'pastry'. The term roulade originates from the French word 'rouler' which means 'roll'. Not only do they make for an excellent pick during dinners and luncheons, these nutrient-rich rolls are a healthy option for school kids as well. You can trick them to eating greens too! Experiment with the fillings and try a new variation each time you make tandoori chicken and spinach roulade. *Important tip: Try to cut the chicken slices as thin as possible.*

These are parcels of happiness wrapped in thin, soft, masala chicken crêpes. This is my comfort food. I remember how my very first batch of thin crêpes had turned out to be a big disaster. But then, with cooking, giving up is never an answer. The joy is to bite into that perfect crêpe after a series of failed attempts. You can master the art only after you have struggled enough. The passion should not die, no matter what!

Chicken Masala Crêpe Parcels

Serves: Makes 10-12 parcels

Ingredients

For the Crêpe

All-purpose flour (*maida*) 1½ cup
Egg 2
Cumin (*jeera*) powder ½ tsp
Black pepper powder ½ tsp
Water 1 cup
Milk ½ cup
Salt to taste

For the Filling

Oil 4 tbsp + 3 tbsp (for frying)
Onion 4 (finely diced)
Green chilli 7 (finely chopped)
Ginger paste 1 tsp
Garlic paste 1 tsp
Tomato 2 (finely diced)
Turmeric (*haldi*) powder ½ tsp
Salt to taste
Chicken 250 gms (pre-cooked & shredded)
Fresh coriander (*dhania*) leaves 3 tbsp, (finely chopped)
Maida slurry (1 tbsp all-purpose flour {*maida*} + 5 tbsp water)

Method

- In a mixer, combine all the ingredients for the crêpe.
- Beat until a smooth, thin batter is formed. Allow the batter to rest for 20 minutes.
- Heat a non-stick pan on medium flame. Pour a big spoonful of batter onto the pan.
- Tilt the pan with a circular motion so that the batter coats the surface evenly.
- Cook the crêpe for a minute, until the sides leave the pan.
- Remove and keep aside on a lightly oiled flat tray.
- Repeat the process till you have used the whole batter.
- In a pan, heat the oil. Add the onions and fry till slightly brown.
- Add the green chillies, ginger-garlic pastes.
- Add the tomatoes, turmeric powder, salt and sauté for a few minutes.
- Add the shredded chicken and coriander leaves. Mix well.
- Remove and keep aside. Let this mixture cool down.
- Put a tablespoon of the chicken in the centre of the crêpe, fold on all the four sides, forming a square. Seal the edge with maida slurry.
- Repeat the same process for all the crêpes.
- Shallow fry these parcels in a non-stick pan, using very little oil until they turn golden brown on both sides. Serve these crêpe parcels with your favourite dip.

Murg Makai Kebabs

(corn and chicken kebabs)

Serves: Makes 20 kebabs

Ingredients

Green chilli 8
Fresh coriander (*dhania*) leaves (a small bunch)
Garlic paste 2 tsp
Ginger paste 2 tsp
Cashew nut powder 5 tbsp
White pepper powder 2 tsp
*Garam masala powder 1 tsp
Egg yolk 1
Cream 4 tbsp
Curd / yoghurt (*dahi*) 4 tbsp
Processed cheese 4 cubes (grated)
Salt to taste
Chicken 500 gms (minced, mix of breast & thigh pieces)
Corn kernels 100 gms (boiled)
Butter 2 tbsp
Oil 3 tbsp

For the Garnishing

Chaat masala ½ tsp
Lemon 1 (cut into wedges)
Onion 2 (sliced)

Method

- Grind the chillies and coriander in a blender to make a coarse paste.
- In a large bowl, mix the prepared paste, all the remaining ingredients with the minced chicken and corn except butter and oil. Mix well till combined.
- Roll the chicken mixture into any shape of your choice.
- Heat the butter and oil in a pan, shallow fry the kebabs for 3-4 minutes on both sides till golden brown and done.
- Sprinkle the chaat masala and squeeze lemon juice over the kebabs as required.
- Serve with onion slices and green chutney.

*For the garam masala powder recipe, refer to page no. 8

How about adding corn to the classic chicken kebabs? This is my variation that I'd like you to try and enjoy. Not only are the spices a house of flavours, the crunchiness of the corn kernels gives an interesting texture to the dish that will definitely catch your fancy. The rich curd blends well with the spices.

If you are a beginner in the kitchen and intend to impress your special someone, then these kebabs could be your best bet. Fried chicken kebabs are best enjoyed when crispy. If given a chance, my kids would love to hog on these kebabs every day. Follow this simple recipe and surprise everyone with your rendition of yet another classic kebab dish!

Fried Chicken Kebabs Serves: 6

Ingredients

Chicken 1 kg (skinless, medium size pieces with bone)

For the Marinade

Ginger paste 1 tbsp
Garlic paste 1 tbsp
Red chilli powder 2 tsp
Black pepper powder 2 tsp
Vinegar 3 tbsp
Lemon juice 2 tbsp
Orange-red food colour ⅛ tsp (optional)
Salt to taste

Other Ingredients

Egg 1
Cornstarch 6 tbsp
Oil for frying

Method

- Wash the chicken and strain the excess water.
- In a bowl, add all the marinade ingredients and mix well.
- Add the chicken pieces to this mix and combine till the chicken is coated evenly.
- Allow to marinate for 2-3 hours.
- Add the egg and cornstarch to the marinated chicken and mix well.
- In a deep pan / kadai, heat the oil, fry the chicken till crispy and done.
- Serve with onion rings and lemon wedges.

Hunan Chicken with Rice and Noodles

Serves: 6

Ingredients

For the Hunan Chicken Gravy

Chicken 400 gms (boneless thigh pieces, cut into thin, long strips)
Egg white 1
Cornstarch 2 tbsp
Salt to taste
Oil 4 tbsp
*Chilli oil 1 tbsp
Ginger 1 tsp (finely chopped)
Garlic 1 tsp (finely chopped)
Long, dry red chilli (*Kashmiri*) 5 (torn into halves)
Onion 1 (diced)
Green capsicum 1 (diced)
**Chicken stock or water 1½ cups
Oyster sauce 4 tbsp
Soya sauce 2 tbsp
Vinegar 1 tbsp
Sugar 1 tsp
White pepper powder ½ tsp
Sesame (*til*) oil ¼ tsp

For the Rice and Noodles

Oil 3 tbsp
Garlic 1 tbsp (finely chopped)
Spring onions ½ cup (green & white part diced)
Cooked rice 2 cups
Cooked noodles 200 gms

Method

- In a bowl, add the chicken, egg white, cornstarch and salt. Mix and allow to marinate for half an hour.
- In a pan, heat 3 tablespoons of oil and fry the chicken till golden in colour. Keep aside.
- In the same pan, heat the remaining 1 tablespoon of oil with 1 tablespoon of chilli oil on high flame.
- Add the ginger, garlic and fry for half a minute. Add the dry chillies, onion and capsicum.
- Add the chicken pieces. Sauté for a minute.
- In a bowl add the stock, oyster sauce, soya sauce, vinegar, salt, sugar and pepper powder.
- Add this mixture to the chicken and cook till a thick gravy is formed.
- Check the seasoning and add salt only if needed. (Note: Sauces contain salt too.)
- Add the sesame oil.
- In a separate pan, heat 3 tablespoons of oil. Fry the garlic till golden brown.
- Add the rice, noodles and toss with spring onions. Serve with the prepared Hunan gravy.

*For the chilli oil recipe, refer to page no. 9

**For the chicken stock recipe, refer to page no. 33

Leftovers can give you the creeps! What do you do when there is some rice from the previous night's party? If the family is not in the mood to eat the same food again, here's what you can do. This is a simple formula and quick to rustle up too. The noodles add zing to the leftover rice. A mishmash of ingredients, a dash of this, a pinch of that and voila: presenting Hunan chicken with rice and noodles. Serve hot!

Murg Haleem

Serves: 8

Ingredients

To Pressure Cook

Broken wheat (*dahlia*) 250 gms (washed)
Water 2 litres
Bengal gram (*chana dal*) ⅓ cup
Green chilli 6 (slit)
Garlic paste ½ tsp
Ginger paste 1 tsp
Clove (*laung*) 3
Cardamom (*elaichi*) 3 pods
Cinnamon (*dalchini*) 2 sticks
Salt to taste

For the Korma

Oil 300 ml
Cinnamon (*dalchini*) 1 stick
Clove (*laung*) 1
Cardamom (*elaichi*) 2 pods
Onion 2 (sliced)
Chicken 1 kg (skinless, medium size pieces with bones)
Garlic paste 3 tsp
Ginger paste 5 tsp
Red chilli powder 1 tsp
Fresh coriander (*dhania*) leaves 2 tbsp (chopped)
Green chilli 6 (slit)
Curd / yoghurt (*dahi*) 300 gms
*Garam masala powder ½ tsp
Salt to taste

Other Ingredients

Potli ka masala 20 gms (optional)
Cashew nuts 50 gms
Almonds 25 gms
Oil ¼ cup
Clarified butter (*ghee*) 2 tbsp
Onion 2 (sliced)
Split black gram (*urad dal*) ¼ cup (soaked for half an hour & blended into a smooth paste)
Lemon juice extracted out of 1 whole lemon
Fried onions, clarified butter (*ghee*), chopped mint and coriander to garnish

Method

- In a pressure cooker, add the broken wheat along with water and the remaining ingredients that have to be pressure cooked. Cook till the wheat and dal are done and allow to cool down.
- To prepare the korma, in a deep pan, heat the oil. Add the cinnamon, clove and cardamom. Add the onions and fry till golden brown.
- Add the chicken pieces, ginger-garlic pastes. Sauté for 3 minutes. Add the red chilli powder, coriander, green chillies, curd, garam masala powder and salt.
- Cook the korma till the chicken is tender. Remove from heat and allow the korma to cool down.
- Remove the chicken pieces, shred them and add the shredded chicken back to the korma.
- Mix the chicken korma to the cooked wheat. Mix well and coarsely blend this mixture.
- Boil the potli ka masala with 1 cup of water for 5 minutes till the water gets infused with the aroma of the herbs (optional). Strain and keep aside.

- Grind the cashew nuts and almonds into a smooth paste.
- To make the haleem, heat a large (heavy-bottomed) pan and add the oil and ghee. Add the onions and fry till golden brown.
- Add the blended chicken and wheat mixture, urad dal paste, nut paste and the infused water.
- Squeeze in the lemon juice. Mix well.
- Cook the haleem for 20 minutes to half an hour on medium-low flame, stirring continuously.
- Garnish with fried onions, ghee, chopped mint, coriander and serve.

*For the garam masala powder recipe, refer to page no. 8

Master this dish with 'labour of love'. The magic ingredient here is the potli ka masala—a mixture of spices, herbs and roots—which gives the haleem its special aromatic fragrance. Unfortunately, it is not easily available. I always buy it in bulk from Hyderabad. Don't fret, even without the masala, the murg haleem will melt-in-your-mouth like a dream.

Biryani is a dish that has innumerable variants, and each version claims its own fan base. The combination of spices is the enduring charm of a well-cooked biryani. What I am sharing here is a take-off of my sister-in-law's (who hails from Hyderabad) recipe. After years of honing this art, I have understood that it's important to strike a balance between time and technique to cook the perfect biryani. There is no room for a single flaw. Follow these easy steps and be a pro at serving a plate of delectable biryani.

Kachee Murg Biryani

Serves: 8

Ingredients

- Cinnamon (*dalchini*) 6 sticks
- Clove (*laung*) 8
- Cardamom (*elaichi*) 8 pods
- Black cumin (*shahi jeera*) ½ tsp
- Oil 1 cup
- Onion 2 (thinly sliced)
- Chicken 1 kg (big pieces with bones)
- Fresh coriander (*dhania*) leaves 30 gms (chopped)
- Mint leaves 15 gms (chopped)
- Green chilli 10 (ground into a paste)
- Ginger paste 2½ tbsp
- Garlic paste 1½ tbsp
- Red chilli powder 2 tsp
- Coriander (*dhania*) powder 1 tsp
- Lemon juice extracted out of 1½ lemons
- Curd / yoghurt (*dahi*) 300 gms (lightly beaten)
- Salt to taste

For the Rice

- Water as required (should be 4-5 times more than the quantity of rice, as the rice will be strained once ¾th cooked)
- Black cumin (*shahi jeera*) ¼ tsp
- Lemon juice extracted out of ½ a lemon
- Salt to taste
- Long grain / Basmati rice 3½ cups (washed & soaked for half an hour)

For the Layering

- Milk ½ cup (add a pinch of yellow food colour & pinch of saffron to this)
- Onion 1 (sliced & deep fried till golden brown)
- Clarified butter (*ghee*) 3 tbsp

Method

- Grind cinnamon, clove, cardamom and black cumin into a powder. Keep aside.
- In a deep pan / kadai, heat the oil and fry the onions till golden brown.
- Strain the fried onions and keep aside, reserving the oil.
- Once the onions cool down, crush them coarsely.
- In a large bowl, add the chicken pieces along with coriander, mint, green chilli paste, ginger-garlic pastes, red chilli powder, coriander powder, lemon juice, curd, prepared powder, oil (in which the onions were fried) and salt.
- Mix well till all the ingredients are combined. Marinate for 2 hours.
- In a large deep pan, heat the water and add black cumin.
- Squeeze in the lemon juice and add salt accordingly.
- When the water comes to a rapid boil, add the rice and cook till the rice is just about ¾th done. Take care not to overcook the rice.

- Remove from heat and strain the water immediately. (Note: Reserve ½ cup of this water.)
- In a heavy-bottomed pan, (the pan should have a wide mouth) add the marinated chicken.
- Add ½ cup of the reserved hot rice water.
- Layer the cooked rice over the marinated chicken and spread evenly.
- With the back of a long spoon make some holes in the rice layer. Pour the milk mixture on it.
- Spoon the ghee over and sprinkle the fried onions on top.
- Cover the pan. Make sure the pan is tightly covered so that the steam does not escape. You can place a heavy object on the pan or seal it with dough.
- Cook on high flame for 20 minutes.
- Keep turning the biryani pan at regular intervals, meanwhile, heat a tawa / flat pan and place the biryani pan on it. Cook on a low flame for 10 minutes.
- To check if the biryani is done, insert the back of a long spoon till it touches the bottom. If it comes out clean and dry when you remove the spoon, the biryani is done. If it has masala sticking on it, continue to cook for a few more minutes.
- Serve with raita and mirchi ka salan.

For the Mirchi Ka Salan

Oil ½ cup
Banana peppers 200 gms (slit vertically on one side without cutting them into half)
Cumin (*jeera*) seeds ½ tsp
Onion ½ (sliced)
Ginger paste 1 tsp
Garlic paste 1 tsp
Red chilli powder ½ tsp
Coriander (*dhania*) powder ½ tsp
Turmeric (*haldi*) powder ¼ tsp
Tamarind (*imli*) 20 gms (soaked in 1 cup of warm water, squeezed & pulp strained)
Salt to taste

For the Masala Paste

Dry coconut 30 gms (grated & dry roasted)
Peanuts 50 gms (roasted)
Sesame (*til*) seeds 2 tbsp (roasted)
Green chilli 6

Method

- Grind the masala paste ingredients until smooth.
- In a pan, heat the oil. Add the banana peppers and fry for 3 minutes.
- Remove and keep aside.
- In the same oil, add cumin seeds and onion. Fry till golden brown.
- Add the ginger-garlic pastes. Sauté for half a minute.
- Add the ground masala paste, along with chilli powder, coriander powder, turmeric powder and sauté for 4 minutes on medium low flame.
- Add the tamarind pulp, fried peppers and salt.
- Simmer for 10 minutes till the peppers become soft and the oil separates.
- Serve with biryani.

Dum Ki Murg

Serves: 4-5

Ingredients

For the White Paste

- Oil 1 tsp
- Dry coconut 1 tbsp (grated)
- Poppy seeds (*khus khus*) 1 tsp
- Chironji (*charoli*) seeds 25 gms
- Cashew nuts 50 gms

For the Marinade

- Oil ½ cup
- Onion 2 (sliced)
- Tomato 1 (very finely diced)
- Fresh coriander (*dhania*) leaves 3 tbsp (freshly chopped)
- Green chilli 7 (ground into a paste)
- Red chilli powder 2 tsp
- Black pepper powder 1 tsp
- Turmeric (*haldi*) powder ¼ tsp
- Garlic paste 1 tbsp
- Ginger paste 1½ tbsp
- Tomato ketchup 2 tbsp
- Lemon juice extracted out of ½ a lemon
- Curd / yoghurt (*dahi*) 250 gms
- *Garam masala powder ½ tsp
- Salt to taste
- Chicken 1 kg (skinless)
- Butter 2 tbsp
- Egg 1 (boiled)

Method

- In a pan, heat the oil on low flame. Add dry grated coconut and roast for half a minute. Remove and keep aside.
- In the same pan, roast the poppy seeds. Be careful not to burn the seeds.
- In a blender, add the roasted coconut, poppy seeds, chironji, cashew nuts with little water and grind into a smooth paste. Keep aside.
- Heat ½ cup of oil and fry the onions till golden brown. Strain the fried onions and keep aside, reserving the oil. Allow the onions to cool down and crush them coarsely.
- In a large bowl, add the ingredients for the marinade along with the crushed fried onions, the reserved oil and mix well. Smear the chicken generously with the marinade.
- Place the chicken along with the extra marinade in a heavy-bottomed pan. Allow to marinate for 2 hours. Place the pan on high flame for 10 minutes. Add the white paste and mix well.
- Cook on medium-low flame for 5 minutes, stirring occasionally.
- Reduce heat, add the butter and cover the pan. Cook on low flame till the chicken is tender and the oil separates. (Keep turning the chicken at regular intervals).
- To serve, stuff the chicken with boiled egg. Garnish with fried onions and chopped coriander.
- Serve with hot naan or rice.

*For the garam masala powder recipe, refer to page no. 8

A stellar dum ki murg dish depends on two factors: good marination and slow cooking. Savour the spice rich gravy with naan, parantha or fragrant ghee rice. For those who prefer not to use the whole chicken, I'd advise you to slice the chicken into big pieces instead.

Cheesy Nachos with Chicken Keema

Serves: 5

Ingredients

For the Nachos Chips

- Maize flour (*makki ka atta*) 1 cup
- All-purpose flour (*maida*) ½ cup
- Chilli flakes 1 tsp
- Oregano 1 tsp
- Salt to taste
- Oil for deep frying

Method

- In a deep bowl, combine all the ingredients except the oil. Add the water accordingly and knead into a soft, stiff dough.
- Roll the dough into thin chapattis. Use some flour for dusting.
- Prick with a fork and cut into triangles.
- In a deep pan, heat the oil. Deep fry the chips on medium-high flame, until golden brown.
- Drain on an absorbent paper and keep aside.
- Repeat the same process to prepare the remaining chips.

For the Keema

- Oil 2 tbsp
- Onion 1 (finely diced)
- Garlic ½ tbsp (finely chopped)
- Red chilli powder 1 tsp
- Coriander (*dhania*) powder ½ tsp
- Black pepper powder ½ tsp
- Cumin (*jeera*) powder 1 tsp
- Dry oregano 1 tsp
- Dry thyme ½ tsp
- Chicken 200 gms (minced)
- Tomato 3 (blanched, skin removed, deseeded & finely chopped)
- Tomato sauce 4 tbsp
- Salt to taste

Method

- In a pan, heat the oil and add onions. Fry till translucent. Add the garlic and sauté till soft.
- Add the chilli powder, coriander powder, pepper powder, cumin powder, oregano, thyme, chicken mince and sauté for 3-4 minutes.
- Add the chopped tomatoes, tomato sauce and salt. Cook for 10 minutes till the keema is done and the mixture is dry.

For the Cheese Sauce

Butter 1 tbsp
All-purpose flour (*maida*) 1 tbsp
Milk 1 cup
Cheese 2 slices
Cheddar cheese 50 gms (grated)
English mustard ½ tsp
Salt to taste
Parsley (a few leaves to garnish)

Method

- In a pan, heat the butter. Add the flour and sauté for 2 minutes on low flame.
- Add the milk gradually and stir continuously with a hand whisk till it slightly thickens.
- Add the cheese slices and Cheddar cheese. Cook for a minute till the cheese melts. Turn off the heat. Add the English mustard and season with salt.
- To assemble, arrange the nachos on a plate and spoon the keema, followed by the cheese sauce. Garnish with parsley leaves and serve immediately.

Keema is the fusion agent here. While the cheese and the nachos guarantee a Mexican culinary affair, the keema promises an explosion of tastes and flavours. By far, this is the most-voted for 'comfort food' dish among youngsters.

Pepper Chicken Steak with Creamy Mashed Potatoes

Serves: 3

Ingredients

For the Pepper Sauce

Oil 1 tbsp
Chicken 250 gms (medium size pieces with bones)
Onion 1 (roughly diced)
Garlic 10 cloves
*Red chilli paste 1 tbsp
Red bell pepper 1 (roughly diced)
Tomato 2 (quartered)
Black peppercorns 1 tsp
Water 3 cups
Butter 2 tbsp
All-purpose flour (*maida*) 1 tbsp
Soya sauce 1 tbsp
English mustard ½ tsp
Tomato ketchup 1 tbsp
Black pepper powder 1 tbsp (freshly crushed)
Vinegar 1 tbsp
Salt to taste

Method

- In a pressure cooker, heat the oil.
- Add the chicken and fry till it turns brown.
- Add onion, garlic, red chilli paste, red bell pepper, tomato, black peppercorns and water.
- Cover and pressure cook for 4 whistles. Reduce flame and cook for 15 minutes.
- Once the pressure drops, open and strain the stock.
- In a separate pan, heat the butter. Add the flour and fry till light brown in colour.
- Add the strained stock gradually and stir briskly with a hand whisk so that no lumps are formed.
- Once it starts boiling, add the soya sauce, English mustard, tomato ketchup, black pepper powder and vinegar. Season with salt.
- Cook till the sauce thickens and keep aside.

*For the red chilli paste recipe, refer to page no. 9

For the Creamy Mashed Potato

Potato 2 (boiled & grated)
Milk 50 ml
Butter 1 tbsp
Chilli flakes ½ tsp
Cream 50 ml
Parsley 2 tbsp (chopped)
Salt to taste

Method

- Blend the potatoes and milk into a smooth mixture.
- In a pan, heat the butter.
- Add the chilli flakes, potato mixture, cream, salt and cook till you get a creamy, smooth sauce.
- Add the parsley. Keep aside.

For the Chicken

Fresh thyme 1 tbsp (chopped)	Olive oil 3 tbsp
Black pepper powder 1 tbsp (freshly crushed)	Salt to taste
Garlic 1 tbsp (finely chopped)	Chicken 400 gms (boneless breast pieces sliced horizontally into half)

Method

- In a bowl, combine thyme, black pepper powder, garlic with 1 tablespoon of olive oil and salt.
- Rub evenly over the chicken breast pieces. Allow to marinate for half an hour.
- In a grill pan, heat the remaining 2 tablespoons of olive oil.
- Fry the chicken on both sides for 4 minutes till golden brown and done.
- To serve, heat the prepared sauce and creamy mashed potatoes.
- Spoon the mashed potatoes on a serving plate, place the fried chicken, pour the pepper sauce on it and serve with grilled or boiled vegetables.

The sharp, spicy flavour of the pepper makes this a must-have dish during winter. It's warm and delightfully delicious. The potatoes of course are a classic favourite, anytime of the year. What I like to do is that I always make extra sauce and preserve it. Whenever my kids pester me for pepper chicken steak with creamy mashed potatoes, I whip up everything like a super mom in no time because I have the sauce ready.

Grilled Chicken with Mexican Rice

Serves: 4-5

Ingredients

Tomato 3 (very finely chopped)
Ginger paste 1 tsp
Garlic paste 1 tsp
Fresh coriander (*dhania*) leaves 3 tbsp (chopped)
Green chilli 3 (chopped)
Lemon juice extracted out of 1 whole lemon
Curd / yoghurt (*dahi*) 200 gms
Red chilli powder 1 tsp
Black pepper powder 1 tsp
Soya sauce 1 tbsp
Salt to taste
Chicken 1 kg (skinless & cut into 4 pieces)
Oil 4 tbsp

Method

- In a deep, large bowl, add the tomatoes along with all the remaining ingredients except for the oil and chicken pieces.
- Mix well and keep mashing the tomatoes till they blend well along with the masala.
- Add the chicken pieces to the masala.
- Refrigerate and allow to marinate for 4 hours or overnight.
- Preheat the oven at 200°C.
- Add oil to the marinated chicken. Place the chicken on a baking tray.
- Cover with aluminium foil. Place the tray in the oven and cook for 45 minutes till the chicken is done and the gravy has thickened.
- To serve, arrange the grilled chicken on a bed of Mexican rice.
- Spoon some thick gravy over. Garnish with chopped coriander and serve.

For the Mexican Rice

Olive oil 2 tbsp
Butter 1 tbsp
Onion 1 (finely diced)
Garlic 1 tbsp (finely chopped)
Rice 2 cups
Tomato paste 2 tbsp
Tomato purée ½ cup
Oregano ½ tsp
*Chicken stock 2 cups
Water 1 cup
Salt to taste
Boiled peas ½ cup
Boiled corn kernels ½ cup

Method

- In a deep pan, heat the oil and butter. Add the onions and garlic.
- Sauté till the onions are translucent.
- Add washed rice and sauté on low flame for 2 minutes.
- Now add the tomato paste, tomato purée, oregano.
- Sauté for a minute and add the stock and water.
- Season with salt. Stir and bring to a boil.
- When the liquid has almost evaporated, add the peas and corn. Mix well.
- Reduce the flame, cover and cook the rice till done.

*For the chicken stock recipe, refer to page no. 33

The Mexican rice here, teamed with crusty corn and tangy tomatoes, is fabulously flavourful and when combined with the chicken, it makes for a hearty meal. The multiple colours on the platter offer a visual treat. It looks just as good as it tastes. Make sure the chicken is slow-cooked in this recipe. The gravy—with its thick consistency—can be relished with rotis as well, though I'd personally go for rice.

Mutton

Tawa chops are my husband's favourite and the rest of my family loves to gorge on these as well. These chops lend an element of spiciness to an otherwise ordinary meal. You can savour these with a simple dal and rice dish. Trust me, it is a great combination!

Tawa Chops

Serves: 4

Ingredients

Mutton chops 500 gms

For the Masala

Onion ½
Fresh coriander (*dhania*) leaves 25 gms, (roughly chopped)
Curry leaves 10 sprigs (use only the leaves)
Black peppercorns 1 tsp
Red chilli powder 2 tsp
Coriander (*dhania*) powder 1 tsp
Cumin (*jeera*) seeds 1 tsp
Vinegar 2 tbsp
Ginger paste 1 tbsp
Garlic paste 1 tbsp
Salt to taste
Oil 2 tbsp (for frying)

Method

- Blend all the masala ingredients into a smooth paste.
- In a bowl, mix the mutton chops with the masala.
- Allow to marinate for half an hour.
- Pressure cook for 3 whistles. The meat should be just about ¾th done.
- When the pressure drops, open the cooker, simmer and cook till the moisture content has reduced and the chops are evenly coated with the masala.
- In a tawa or a non-stick pan, heat the oil.
- Fry the chops till golden brown on both sides and cooked completely.
- Serve with onion rings and lemon wedges.

Keema Koftas

Serves: Makes 20 koftas

Ingredients

Mutton 500 gms (minced, washed & excess water strained)
Oil 2 tbsp

For the Masala

Onion 1 (small-sized & roughly chopped)
Garlic 10 cloves
Fresh coriander (*dhania*) leaves 25 gms
Green chilli 6
Red chilli powder 2 tsp
Coriander (*dhania*) powder ½ tsp
Turmeric (*haldi*) powder ½ tsp
Black peppercorns ¼ tsp
Roasted Bengal gram (*bhuna chana / phutana dal*) ⅓ cup
Fresh coconut 70 gms (grated)
Salt to taste
Oil (for deep frying the koftas)

Method

- Grind all the masala ingredients into a paste.
- Remove in a bowl and keep aside.
- Coarsely grind the keema with 2 tablespoons of oil.
- In a large bowl, mix the masala paste and the keema till well combined.
- Refrigerate for half an hour.
- Shape the koftas into small round balls.
- Fry the koftas in hot oil until golden brown.
- Serve.

Straight from my mother's kitchen, to yours: Keema koftas would be treated as a festival dish during Bakra Eid. Usually served at breakfast, my childhood memories of devouring these soft and juicy koftas have not faded away.

Isn't it hard to refuse a platter of succulent shami kebabs? What if I were to tell you that adding coconut enhances the divine taste and gives these kebabs a beautiful texture? Do not miss out on this flavourful version. Try it without further delay.

Shami Kebabs

Serves: Makes 20 kebabs

Ingredients

- Mutton 500 gms (minced, washed & strained)
- Tomato 2 (diced)
- Onion 1 (sliced)
- Fresh coconut 50 gms (grated)
- Green chilli 5 (roughly chopped)
- Red chilli powder 2 tsp
- Coriander (*dhania*) powder 1 tsp
- Turmeric (*haldi*) powder ½ tsp
- *Garam masala powder ½ tsp
- Garlic 10 cloves
- Fresh coriander (*dhania*) leaves 2 tbsp (roughly chopped)
- Bengal gram (*chana dal*) ½ cup (washed)
- Salt to taste
- Water 1½ cups
- Egg 1 (use only the white part)
- Oil for deep frying

Method

- In a large bowl, add the minced mutton with all the other ingredients except water, egg and oil. Mix well.
- Add the water and cook this mixture in a pressure cooker for about 3-4 whistles.
- Open the pressure cooker and cook the mixture till completely dry.
- Let this mixture cool down.
- Grind the mixture into a smooth paste.
- Remove in a bowl.
- Add the egg white and mix well.
- To shape the kebabs, divide the mixture into small portions, shape into round balls and flatten them.
- Deep fry till golden brown.
- Serve hot with mint chutney.

*For the garam masala powder recipe, refer to page no. 8

Sukha Fried Mutton Kebabs

Serves: 6-8

Ingredients

Mutton 1 kg (boneless cubes, washed & strained)
Baking soda ¼ tsp

For the Masala

Garlic paste 1½ tbsp
Ginger paste 1 tbsp
Red chilli powder 3 tbsp
Turmeric (*haldi*) powder ½ tsp
Black pepper powder ½ tbsp
Lemon juice extracted out of 3 whole lemons
All-purpose flour (*maida*) 2 tbsp
Rice flour 1 tbsp
Oil for deep frying
Fried curry leaves and slit green chillies to garnish

Method

- Wrap the mutton cubes in a muslin cloth, press and remove excess water.
- Sprinkle the soda and mix well.
- In a bowl, mix all the masala ingredients.
- Add the mutton cubes and mix well.
- Marinate for 2 hours or overnight for best results.
- In a deep pan / kadai, heat the oil.
- Deep fry the kebabs on medium-high flame till golden brown and done.
- Garnish with a few fried curry leaves and slit the green chillies along with some lemon wedges. Serve.

These are super easy to make and taste delicious. I usually tend to prepare in large quantities and store them in airtight bags and fry whenever needed. Sukha fried mutton kebabs make for an excellent evening snack option and can come to the rescue when guests land up unannounced. Put them in the freezer and you can easily stock them for up to two months.

Shahi Zaffrani Gosht Pulao

Serves: 6-8

Ingredients

For the Mutton Gravy

Oil ½ cup	Mutton 1 kg (boneless shoulder pieces)
Onion 6 (sliced)	Red chilli powder 2 tsp
Tomato 4 (finely chopped)	*Garam masala powder ½ tsp
Ginger paste 1 tbsp	Honey 1 tbsp
Garlic paste 1 tbsp	Salt to taste

Method

- In a pan, heat the oil.
- Add the onions and fry till golden brown.
- Remove some of the fried onions and keep aside for garnishing.
- Add the chopped tomatoes, ginger-garlic pastes and fry for a few minutes.
- Add the mutton and fry for 5 minutes.
- Add the chilli powder, garam masala powder, honey and salt.
- Pressure cook till the mutton is done (approximately for 4 whistles).
- When the pressure drops, open the cooker and cook on low flame till the gravy turns semi thick.

For the Saffron Pulao

Oil ¼ cup	Salt to taste
Cumin (*jeera*) seeds ½ tsp	Basmati rice 4 cups (washed & soaked for half an hour)
Green cardamom (*chhoti elaichi*) 2 pods	Saffron (*kesar*) ½ tsp (soaked in 2 tbsp of warm milk)
Cinnamon (*dalchini*) 1-inch stick	
Onion ½ (sliced)	
Water 8 cups	

For Garnishing

Egg 3 (boiled)	Mint leaves 1 tbsp (chopped)
Fried potato wedges (a few)	Onions ¼ cup (fried)
Fresh coriander (*dhania*) leaves 3 tbsp (chopped)	

Method

- In a pan, heat the oil.
- Add the cumin seeds, cardamom, cinnamon and fry for half a minute.
- Add the onion and fry till translucent.
- Add the water, salt and bring to a boil.
- Add the soaked rice and cook till the water has evaporated.
- Reduce the flame and sprinkle the saffron and milk mixture on the rice.
- Cover and cook till the rice is done.
- To serve, first make a layer of rice on the serving dish. Top this layer with the mutton gravy.
- Garnish with fried onions, mint and coriander.
- Serve along with boiled eggs and potato wedges.

*For the garam masala powder recipe, refer to page no. 8

This is one pulao recipe that you can master in no time! My diners think much labour has gone into its making. Surprisingly, it involves no sweat-inducing method.

Dal Gosht with Brown Rice

Serves: 6

Ingredients

Mutton 500 gms (medium size pieces)
Bengal gram (*chana dal*) ⅓ cup
Pigeon peas (*toor dal / arhar dal*) ⅓ cup
Onion 2 (finely diced)
Ginger paste ½ tbsp
Garlic paste ½ tbsp
Red chilli powder 2 tsp
Coriander (*dhania*) powder 1 tsp
Turmeric (*haldi*) powder ½ tsp
*Garam masala powder ¼ tsp
Tomato 3 (finely chopped)
Fresh coriander (*dhania*) leaves 2 tbsp (finely chopped)
Lemon juice extracted out of 1 whole lemon

Method

- In a pressure cooker, add both the dal with 1½ cups of water and turmeric powder.
- Cook till the dal is done (approximately for 5 whistles). Remove from heat.
- Once the pressure drops, open the cooker and purée the dal. Keep aside.
- In a pressure cooker, heat the oil. Add the onion and fry till golden brown.
- Add the mutton pieces and fry for 4 minutes.
- Add the ginger-garlic pastes, chilli powder, coriander powder and tomatoes.
- Fry till the tomatoes become soft.
- Add the coriander leaves. Season with salt.
- Add 1 cup of water and pressure cook till the mutton is done (approximately for 4 whistles).
- Once the pressure drops, open the cooker and add the puréed dal to the mutton. Bring to a boil. Add the lemon juice.
- Serve.

For the Brown Rice

Basmati rice 2 cups (washed & soaked in water for half an hour)
Sugar 1 tbsp
Oil 2 tbsp
Onion 1 (sliced)
Cumin (*jeera*) seeds 1 tsp
Clove (*laung*) 6
Cinnamon (*dalchini*) 1 stick
Cardamom (*elaichi*) 4 pods
Black peppercorns 6
Salt to taste
Water 4 cups

*For the garam masala powder recipe, refer to page no. 8

Method

- In a pan, add the sugar and allow to caramelise till golden brown.
- Add 1 cup of water. Bring to a boil and keep aside.
- In a deep pot, heat the oil. Add the onions and fry till golden brown.
- Add the remaining spices. Sauté for half a minute.
- Add the remaining 3 cups of water, the sugar-infused water and salt. Bring to a boil.
- Add the rice and cook on high flame till the water evaporates.
- Reduce the flame, cover and cook till the rice is done.
- Serve rice with dal gosht.

Lentils and meat make a delectable pair. The sugar in the rice assures a subtle sweetness and gives a lovely brown colour. The sugar also helps balancing the play of spices in the meat. This lentil-rich dish is a wholesome, healthy meal.

Hari Gosht Ki Phal (Green Mutton curry)

Serves: 6

Ingredients

Oil 4 tbsp
Onion 1 (sliced)
Mutton 500 gms (medium size pieces)
Red chilli powder ½ tsp
Ginger paste 1 tsp
Garlic paste 1 tsp
Black pepper powder 1 tsp (freshly crushed)
Tomato 1 (diced)
Salt to taste
Lemon juice extracted out of 1 whole lemon
Water ½ cup

For the Green Masala

Fresh coriander (*dhania*) leaves 100 gms
Green chilli 10

Method

- Grind the green masala ingredients into a smooth paste.
- In a pressure cooker, heat the oil.
- Add the onions and fry till translucent.
- Add the mutton and fry for 4 minutes.
- Add the chilli powder, ginger-garlic pastes, black pepper powder and tomatoes.
- Sauté for 2 minutes and then add the green masala and salt.
- Sauté till the raw smell disappears, for about 5 minutes, on low flame.
- Add the lemon juice along with ½ cup of water.
- Pressure cook till the mutton is done.
- Serve the hot gravy with paranthas.

The freshness of the coriander leaves and the spicy green chillies combine to make one gorgeous-looking dish! You can follow the same recipe with chicken as well. Relish the finger-licking goodness of what I'd like to call this beauty, Hari gosht ki phal.

Lal Masala Phal with Khatta Khana (Red Mutton Gravy with Tamarind Rice)

Serves: 6-8

Ingredients

For the Lal Masala Phal

Oil 2 tbsp
Ginger paste 1 tsp
Garlic paste 1 tsp
Red chilli powder 1 tsp
Mutton 500 gms (medium size pieces)
Water ½ cup
Salt to taste

For the Masala

Onion 1 (roughly chopped)
Black peppercorns ½ tbsp
Clove (*laung*) 3
Cinnamon (*dalchini*) 1 stick

Method

- In a blender, grind the masala ingredients into a smooth paste.
- In a pressure cooker, heat the oil. Add the ginger-garlic pastes. Sauté for a half a minute.
- Add the chilli powder, masala paste and sauté till the raw smell disappears, for 4 minutes on medium flame. Add the mutton pieces, mix well with the masala. Cook for 5 minutes.
- Add ¼ cup of water, salt and pressure cook till the mutton is soft and properly done (approximately for 4 whistles). Open the cooker. Cook till the gravy is thick.

For the Tamarind Rice

Cumin (*jeera*) seeds 1 tbsp
Fenugreek (*methi*) seeds ½ tsp
Mustard (*rai*) seeds 1 tbsp
Bengal gram (*chana dal*) 1 tbsp
Split black gram (*urad dal*) 1 tbsp
Oil ½ cup
Peanuts ¼ cup
Sesame (*til*) seeds 2 tbsp
Dry coconut ½ cup (grated)
Garlic 4 cloves (crushed)
Long, dry red chilli (*Kashmiri*) 4 (broken into halves)
Asafoetida (*hing*) ¹/₈ tsp or a pinch
Red chilli powder 1 tbsp
Turmeric (*haldi*) powder ½ tsp
Tamarind (*imli*) 80 gms (soaked in 2 cups of water for half an hour, squeezed & pulp removed)
Salt to taste
Water as required
Rice 1½ cups (washed & soaked for 10 minutes)

Method

- Dry roast cumin, fenugreek, mustard, ½ tablespoon of Bengal gram and ½ tablespoon of split black gram. Allow to cool down and grind into a powder.

- In a deep pan, heat the oil. Fry the peanuts. Add sesame seeds, dry grated coconut, garlic, dry red chillies, the remaining Bengal gram and split black gram; asafoetida, red chilli powder and turmeric.
- Add the prepared powder to this mix and fry for a minute.
- Add the tamarind pulp and salt, cook this mixture till the oil separates and it achieves a slightly thick consistency. Keep aside.
- In a pot, bring the water to a rapid boil. Add the rice and salt.
- Cook till the rice is ¾th done and strain the excess water.
- Next, add the tamarind masala mixture with the rice. Mix well.
- Cover and cook till the rice is fully done.

Keema Parcels

Serves: Makes 20 parcels

Ingredients

For the Dough

All-purpose flour (*maida*) 2 cups
Salt to taste
Oil ¼ cup (warmed)
Milk 1 cup (warmed)
Maida slurry (1 tbsp all-purpose flour {*maida*} + 5 tbsp water)

For the Keema Filling

Mutton 150 gms (minced, washed & excess water strained)
Green peas 50 gms (parboiled)
Onion 2 (medium-sized & sliced)
Fresh coriander (*dhania*) leaves 3 tbsp, (finely chopped)
Green chilli 3 (finely chopped)
Ginger paste ½ tsp
Garlic paste ½ tsp
Turmeric (*haldi*) powder ¼ tsp
*Garam masala powder (a pinch)
Salt to taste
Oil 2 tbsp + for frying

Method

- In a mixing bowl, place the flour and add salt.
- Make a well in the centre and add the warm oil.
- Mix with the flour till a breadcrumb-like texture is achieved.
- Gradually, add the warm milk as required and knead into a stiff dough. Cover and keep aside.
- In a large bowl, add the minced mutton with all the remaining ingredients except oil.
- Mix well and season with salt.
- In a pan, heat the oil. Sauté the mince mixture on high flame and cook for 6 minutes till the mince is cooked and the mixture is dry.
- Remove into a bowl and allow the mixture to cool down.
- Divide the dough into 6 balls. Roll each ball into a circle (5 cm thick) and cut into squares.
- Spoon the filling on to the centre of the square.
- Seal with another square by putting a little maida slurry on the edges.
- Press the edges properly and crimp the edges with a fork to form a pattern.
- Follow the same process to prepare the remaining parcels.
- Deep fry on medium flame till golden brown.
- Serve hot with mint and raisin chutney.

Little parcels stuffed with lip smacking keema are bundles of joy. The flakiness of the pastry makes the dish crunchy, biscuity and wonderfully crumbly. I have given a twist to the regular mint chutney in this recipe by adding raisins. These parcels can also be baked and you can also experiment with different fillings.

For the Mint and Raisin Chutney

- Fresh coconut 2 tbsp (grated)
- Mint leaves 30 gms
- Fresh coriander (*dhania*) leaves 10 gms
- Tamarind (*imli*) 1 (small, marble-sized ball)
- Green chilli 1
- Cumin (*jeera*) seeds ¼ tsp
- Raisins 2 tbsp (soaked in water)
- Salt to taste

Method

- In a blender, grind all the ingredients into a smooth chutney.

*For the garam masala powder recipe, refer to page no. 8

Simplicity has no substitute and this humble dish proves it like no other kebab variety. Chapli kebabs can be made with simple spices and readily available ingredients. Surprise yourself and everybody else!

Chapli Kebabs

Serves: Makes 15 kebabs

Ingredients

Mutton 500 gms (minced)
Long, dry red chilli (*Kashmiri*) 8 (ground into a paste)
Ginger paste 1½ tsp
Garlic paste 1 tsp
Black pepper powder ½ tsp
Red chilli powder ½ tsp
Tomato 2 (deseeded & very finely diced)
Onion 2 (very finely diced)
Fresh coriander (*dhania*) leaves 4 tbsp (very finely chopped)
Green chilli 2 (very finely chopped)
Egg whites 2
*Special garam masala powder ½ tsp
Salt to taste
Oil 5 tbsp (for frying)

Method

- In a mixer, coarsely grind the keema. Be careful not to make a fine paste.
- In a bowl, add the minced meat and all the remaining ingredients except the oil. Mix well.
- Divide the mixture and shape into round balls and flatten them, slightly bigger than your palm size (6-7 inches).
- Place the kebabs on a tray and freeze them (this helps maintain the shape of the kebabs and avoid breaking).
- In a frying pan, heat the oil.
- Shallow fry the frozen kebabs, first, on high flame and then on low flame, till they are cooked on both sides and are golden brown.
- Serve hot with green chutney and a simple onion and tomato salad.

*For the special garam masala powder recipe, refer to page no. 8

Seekh Kebabs

Serves: 8

Ingredients

Mint leaves 30 gms
Fresh coriander (*dhania*) leaves 10 gms
Oil 2 tbsp
Mutton 500 gms (minced)

For the Masala

Green chilli 6
Onion 2 (sliced)
Cashew nuts 70 gms
Roasted Bengal gram (*bhuna chana / phutana dal*) 60 gms
Garlic paste 1 tbsp
Ginger paste 1½ tbsp
Cumin (*jeera*) seeds ½ tbsp
Black peppercorns 1 tsp
Cardamom (*elaichi*) 2 pods
Cinnamon (*dalchini*) 2 sticks
Clove (*laung*) 3
Allspice (*kabab chini*) 5 pods
*Special garam masala powder 1 tsp
Oil 6 tbsp
Salt to taste

Method

- In a food processor or chopper, coarsely chop the mint and coriander leaves.
- In a blender, grind all the masala ingredients except the oil into a smooth paste. Add the mince and pulse briefly. Keep aside.
- In a large bowl, mix the mince with the chopped mint, coriander and oil.
- Mix well and refrigerate for 2 hours or overnight.
- To shape the kebabs, wet your hands with a little water or oil them. Take some mince mixture and give it a sausage-like shape.
- Microwave these kebabs for a minute on both sides.
- In a pan, heat 4 tablespoons of oil and shallow fry the kebabs till golden brown on both sides.
- Serve these piping hot kebabs with onion rings and mint chutney.

*For the special garam masala powder recipe, refer to page no. 8

The most popular and utterly delicious, seekh kebab is the quintessential Indian appetiser. With the warm profusion of many spices, this dish is a winter must-have. Roll the spicy kebabs in a rumali roti and feast like a king!

As the name suggests, chilli is the hero here. Since the green chillies are the only source of spiciness, it is a simple dish that does not confuse the palate with too many flavours. Hog till you drop!

Chilli Mutton

Serves: 5

Ingredients

Mutton 500 gms (boneless & cubed)
Green chilli 7 (slit into halves)
Ginger paste 1 tsp
Garlic paste 1 tsp
Black pepper powder ½ tsp
Vinegar 4 tbsp
Salt to taste
Water ½ cup
Oil 3 tbsp
Onion 2 (finely diced)
Soya sauce 2 tbsp
Tomato ketchup 1 tbsp
Fresh coriander (*dhania*) leaves 20 gms, (finely chopped)

Method

- In a bowl, add the mutton pieces along with green chillies, ginger-garlic pastes, pepper powder, vinegar and salt.
- Mix well and allow to marinate for half an hour.
- Add ½ cup of water and pressure cook till the mutton is done. Make sure the mutton is not overcooked.
- In a pan, heat the oil.
- Fry the onions till translucent.
- Add the cooked mutton along with the stock and bring to a boil.
- Add the soya sauce, tomato ketchup, coriander and cook the mutton till it gets evenly coated with the masala.
- Season with salt.
- If you want the mutton to taste spicier, add a few more green chillies.
- Garnish with coriander leaves.
- Serve.

Crispy Sesame Mutton

Serves: 5

Ingredients

Black pepper powder 1 tsp
Tabasco chilli sauce 1 tsp
Oil 1 tbsp
Salt to taste
Mutton 500 gms (boneless, cut into thin strips)
Flour mix for dry coating (50 gms all-purpose flour {*maida*}, 50 gms cornstarch, ½ tsp black pepper powder & salt)
Oil for frying
Red bell pepper ½ (sliced)
Green bell pepper ½, (sliced)
Yellow bell pepper ½, (sliced)
Sesame (*til*) seeds 2 tbsp (roasted)
Iceberg lettuce (a few leaves)

For the Sauce

Oil 2 tbsp
Garlic 1 tsp (finely chopped)
Ginger 1 tsp (grated)
Star anise 2
*Red chilli paste 2 tbsp
Soya sauce 5 tbsp
Tomato sauce 2 tbsp
Vinegar 1 tbsp
Light brown sugar 2 tbsp
Water ¼ cup
Salt to taste

Method

- In a bowl, add the pepper powder, chilli sauce, oil, salt and the mutton strips.
- Mix well and allow to marinate for 2 hours.
- In a separate bowl, add the flour mix and the marinated mutton strips.
- Mix well till the flour has evenly coated the mutton strips.
- In a wok / kadai, heat the oil and deep fry the mutton strips in batches till golden brown. Keep aside.
- In a separate pan, heat the oil.
- Add the ginger, garlic and star anise and fry for a minute.
- Next, add all the remaining ingredients.
- Season with salt and cook till the mixture achieves a thick sauce-like consistency.
- Now, add the fried mutton along with the red, yellow and green peppers. Mix well.
- Serve the mutton on a bed of lettuce leaves.
- Sprinkle the sesame seeds on top.

*For the red chilli paste recipe, refer to page no. 9

The crispiness of the sesame seeds adds a lovely texture to this dish. The sweet and spicy sauces even out the flavours very well. Sitting on a bed of lettuce, crispy sesame mutton is an absolute stunner! Let this be your special offering on the menu the next time you don the hat of a party planner.

Seafood

This dish brings with it a kind of coastal comfort that will instantly make you happy. These deep-fried crisp prawns taste supremely delicious. The fresh coconut in this recipe is an added bonus.

Coconut Crusted Prawns

Serves: 5

Ingredients

Prawns 400 gms (shell removed, deveined, tails intact & washed)
Garlic paste 1 tbsp
Black pepper powder 1 tsp
Turmeric (*haldi*) powder ½ tsp
Vinegar 1 tbsp
Salt to taste
Egg whites 2
Cornstarch 2½ tbsp
Breadcrumbs 1 cup
Fresh coconut ½ cup (grated)
Oil for deep frying

Method

- In a large bowl, add the prawns with garlic paste, black pepper powder, turmeric powder, vinegar and salt.
- Mix well and marinate for half an hour.
- In a separate bowl, lightly whisk the egg whites and cornstarch till well combined.
- In a plate, mix the breadcrumbs and the grated coconut.
- In a deep pan, heat the oil.
- Dip each prawn into the egg white mixture.
- Roll in the breadcrumbs and coconut mixture.
- Repeat the process with all the remaining prawns.
- Deep fry in hot oil till the prawns are crisp and golden brown.
- Serve with tartar sauce.

For the Tartar Sauce

Dill leaves 1 tbsp (finely chopped)
Pickled gherkins 1 tbsp (drained & finely chopped)
Capers 1 tbsp (drained & finely chopped)
Garlic ½ tsp (finely chopped)
Lemon juice 1 tsp
Black pepper powder ½ tsp
Mayonnaise 6 tbsp
Salt to taste

Method

- In a bowl, mix all the ingredients.
- Chill before serving.

Prawn Ghee Roast

Serves: 5

Ingredients

Prawns 400 gms (shell removed, deveined & washed)

For the Marinade

Curd / yoghurt (*dahi*) ½ cup
Red chilli powder 1 tsp
Turmeric (*haldi*) powder ½ tsp
Lemon juice 1 tbsp
Salt to taste

For the Chilli Masala

Byadagi chilli 8
Long, dry red chilli (*Kashmiri*) 5
Coriander (*dhania*) seeds 1 tsp
Cumin (*jeera*) seeds ½ tsp
Fenugreek (*methi*) seeds ½ tsp
Garlic 20 cloves
Tamarind (*imli*) (a small marble-sized ball soaked in ¼ cup of warm water & pulp extracted)
Clarified butter (*ghee*) 5 tbsp
Jaggery (*gud*) 1 tsp (grated)
Curry leaves 10

Method

- In a bowl, add the prawns and the marinade ingredients.
- Mix well and marinate for one hour.
- Boil the dry chillies and allow them to cool down. Keep aside.
- Dry roast the coriander, cumin and fenugreek.
- Grind the soaked chillies along with the roasted spices, garlic and tamarind pulp into a smooth paste.
- In a pan, heat 3 tablespoons of ghee.
- Fry the prawns for about half a minute on both sides.
- Remove the prawns and keep aside.
- In the same pan, add the prepared chilli masala and fry for a minute.
- Add the jaggery, curry leaves and fry for about 5 minutes on low flame, till the ghee separates from the masala.
- Add the cooked prawns back to the masala.
- Add the remaining 2 tablespoons of ghee. Mix well and cook for 3 minutes.
- Serve hot with appams or rotis.

I use Byadagi chillies here, a variety of chilli mainly grown in Karnataka. Prawn ghee roast owes a lot to these chillies for its distinct taste and flavour. Feel free to use long, dry red (Kashmiri) chillies if you find it difficult to get hold of Byadagi chillies. You can follow the same recipe with chicken as well. Important tip: Instead of oil, use ghee. This will add to the richness of this dish.

This is a beautiful, tangy curry that I promise will leave you smacking your lips for another bite. I usually use seer fish, but you can go for any fish of your choice. Macchi ka khatta is enjoyed best with steamed rice. All fish lovers, rejoice!

Macchi Ka Khatta (Fish curry) Serves: 5

Ingredients

Oil 6 tbsp
Onion 1 (small-sized & sliced)
Red chilli powder 2 tsp
Turmeric (*haldi*) powder ½ tsp
Water 2 cups
Seer fish 500 gms (fillets)
Tamarind (*imli*) (a small lemon-sized ball soaked in ¼ cup of water and pulp extracted)
Green chilli 4 (slit)
Salt to taste

For the Masala Paste

Onion 1 (chopped)
Fresh coriander (*dhania*) leaves 4 tbsp (chopped)
Garlic paste 1 tbsp
Cumin (*jeera*) seeds 1 tsp
Fenugreek (*methi*) seeds ¼ tsp
Tomato 5 (chopped)
Fresh coconut ½ cup (grated)

Method

- In a blender, grind all the masala ingredients into a smooth paste.
- In a pan, heat the oil.
- Add the sliced onion and fry till golden brown.
- Add chilli powder, turmeric powder and the prepared masala paste.
- Fry for 6 minutes, till the raw smell disappears and the oil separates from the mixture.
- Add 2 cups of water, tamarind pulp, green chillies, salt, and let the gravy come to a boil.
- Reduce the flame and add the fish slices.
- Cover and cook for 6 minutes till the fish is cooked.
- Serve hot with steamed rice.

Crab Masala

Serves: 5

Ingredients

Oil ¼ cup	Tomato ketchup 2 tbsp
Onion 1 (finely diced)	Vinegar 1 tbsp
Garlic 1 tbsp (finely chopped)	Salt to taste
Curry leaves 20	Crab 1 kg (cleaned)
Green chilli 2 (chopped)	Water 2 cups
Soya sauce 1 tbsp	

For the Masala Paste

Long, dry red chilli (*Kashmiri*) 15 (soaked in hot water for 20 minutes)	Turmeric (*haldi*) powder (a pinch)
Garlic 6 cloves	Onion 1 (chopped)
Coriander (*dhania*) seeds ¼ tsp	Tamarind (*imli*) (a small marble-sized ball soaked in hot water & pulp extracted)

Method

- In a blender, grind the masala paste ingredients until smooth, adding a little warm water as required to assist in grinding.
- In a deep pan, heat the oil. Add the onions and fry till golden brown.
- Add the garlic and fry for a minute.
- Add the curry leaves, green chillies and sauté for half a minute.
- Reduce the flame and add the prepared masala paste. Sauté till the raw smell disappears.
- Add the soya sauce, tomato ketchup and vinegar.
- Season with salt.
- Add the crab and mix well, till the masala has evenly coated the crabs.
- Add the water and cook the crabs for 20 minutes, till done. The masala should be of semi-thick consistency.
- Serve hot with appams or steamed rice.

The sweetness of the crab blends with the spices and sauces like a dream. Words would fail me if I try describing how delicious this dish tastes. It works well as a course by itself but can be savoured with freshly made hot appams or steamed rice. Once you put this dish on the table, all conversations shall cease and everyone will flock to the platter of crab masala.

The smokiness of the grilled peppers and the combination of herbs support the fish to draw in all the flavours. In this recipe, I have used Indian salmon/raavas fish. You can of course pick a variety of your choice.

Fish with Grilled Pepper and Coriander Sauce

Serves: 5

Ingredients

For the Sauce

Red bell pepper 1
Fresh coriander (*dhania*) leaves 25 gms
Parsley leaves 10 gms
Olive oil 6 tbsp
Lemon juice extracted out of 2 whole lemons
Dry oregano 1 tsp
Garlic 1 tbsp (very finely chopped)
Chilli flakes 1 tsp
Salt to taste

Other Ingredients

Black pepper 1 tsp (freshly crushed)
All-purpose flour (*maida*) 1 tbsp
Indian salmon 500 gms (boneless fillets)
Oil 2 tbsp (for frying the fish)

Method

- Spread some oil on the red bell pepper and grill on the stove till completely charred.
- Allow the pepper to cool down and remove the skin. Chop into small dices.
- In a food processor, add coriander, parsley leaves and coarsely chop.
- In a bowl, add the olive oil, grilled pepper, chopped coriander and parsley, lemon juice, oregano, garlic, chilli flakes and salt. Mix well.
- Sprinkle salt, black pepper and flour on both sides of the fish fillets
- In a grill pan, heat the oil.
- Fry the fish till golden brown on both sides.
- Serve the grilled fish with generous amounts of sauce.

Achari Machli

Serves: 6

Ingredients

For the Masala Powder

Cumin (*jeera*) seeds 2 tsp
Mustard (*rai*) seeds 1 tsp
Fenugreek (*methi*) seeds ¼ tsp

For the Marinade

Gram flour (*besan*) 2 tbsp
Ginger paste ½ tsp
Garlic paste ½ tsp
Red chilli powder 1 tsp
Salt to taste

Other Ingredients

Fish 400 gms (boneless & cubed)
Oil 6 tbsp
Garlic 6 cloves (crushed)
Long, dry red chilli (*Kashmiri*) 2 (broken into half)
Curry leaves 10
Onion 1 (diced into big cubes)
Tomato 2 (diced into big cubes)
Prepared masala powder 2 tsp
Lemon juice extracted out of 1 whole lemon
Salt to taste

Method

- Dry roast the masala powder ingredients and grind them into a powder.
- Store in an airtight container and use as required.
- In a bowl, add the marinade ingredients and mix well.
- Add the fish cubes, mix well and marinate for 20 minutes.
- In a pan, heat 4 tablespoons of oil. Fry the fish and keep aside.
- In a separate pan, heat the remaining oil.
- Add the garlic and fry till golden brown.
- Add the red chillies and curry leaves.
- Add the fried fish cubes, onions and tomatoes.
- Sauté on high flame for a minute.
- Add the masala powder and lemon juice. Season with salt.
- Toss for half a minute. Serve immediately.

Who doesn't love a good pickle? The overwhelming spices that go into making a pickle is something we Indians relish with great pleasure; after all it erases the blandness of an everyday, ordinary, regular meal. The pickle masala used here gives an extra delightful kick to the machli.

Fish Cakes with Pineapple and Cherry Tomato Relish

Serves: Makes 20 cakes

Ingredients

For the Fish Cakes

Fish 300 gms (boneless fillets)	Ginger paste ½ tsp
Water ½ cup	Garlic paste ½ tsp
Turmeric (*haldi*) powder ¼ tsp	Green chillies 1 tbsp (finely chopped)
Butter 2 tbsp	Fresh coriander (*dhania*) leaves 3 tbsp (finely chopped)
Oil 6 tbsp	Bread 6 slices
Onion 2 (finely diced)	Salt to taste

Method

- Place the fish fillets in a pan with water.
- Add the turmeric, salt and bring to a boil. Cook for about 4 minutes till the fish is done.
- Remove the pieces and shred them. Reserve the stock.
- In a pan, heat the butter with 1 tablespoon of oil.
- Add the onions and fry till translucent.
- Add the ginger-garlic pastes and fry for a minute.
- Add the chillies, coriander and the shredded fish.
- Season with salt and sauté for 3 minutes.
- Remove the mixture in a bowl and allow it to cool down.
- Soak the bread pieces in the reserved stock and add to this mixture. Mix well.
- Make small balls out of the mixture and flatten them into cakes.
- In a pan, heat the remaining 5 tablespoons of oil and shallow fry the cakes till golden brown on both sides.

For the Pineapple and Cherry Tomato Relish

Oil 2 tbsp	Brown sugar 2 tbsp
Cinnamon (*dalchini*) 2 sticks	Cherry tomatoes 150 gms (quartered)
Cumin (*jeera*) seeds ½ tsp	Ripe pineapple 50 gms (cubed)
Garlic ½ tsp (finely chopped)	Vinegar 1 tsp
Chilli flakes 1 tsp	Salt to taste
Red chilli powder ½ tsp	Spring onions 3 tbsp (chopped)

Method

- In a pan, heat the oil.
- Add the cinnamon sticks, cumin and garlic.
- Fry till the garlic turns golden brown.
- Add the chilli flakes, chilli powder, brown sugar, cherry tomatoes, pineapple and cook till the tomatoes become soft and the mixture turns thick (but chunky).
- Add the vinegar and season with salt.
- Remove from heat and add the spring onions.
- Serve with fish cakes.

The assembly of flavours is noteworthy in this dish. Bread plays an important role here for it gives the fish patties a brilliant texture. The tanginess of cherry tomatoes and the sweetness of pineapple will definitely leave your taste buds tingling!

This is such an easy recipe that even kids can try a hand at making it. I have used simple spices, keeping the flavours uncomplicated and letting the taste of the fish come out in all its delicious glory. An excellent starter, pomfret fry is a dish that can enrich a plain dal curry.

Pomfret Fry

Serves: 3

Ingredients

White pomfret 500 gms

For the Masala

Lemon juice extracted out of 1 whole lemon
Vinegar ½ tbsp
Red chilli powder 1½ tbsp
Coriander (*dhania*) powder ½ tbsp
Black pepper powder ½ tsp
Cumin (*jeera*) powder ½ tsp
Rice flour 1 tbsp
Salt to taste
Oil for frying

Method

- In a large bowl, mix the masala ingredients.
- If the masala is very thick, add 2 tablespoons of water to make the mix thinner.
- Coat the fish with the masala and marinate for an hour.
- In a pan, heat the oil.
- Fry the fish on both sides till done.
- Serve.

Chilli Basil Prawns Serves: 5

Ingredients

Egg white 1
Cornstarch 2 tbsp
Salt to taste
Prawns 500 gms (shell removed, deveined, tails intact & washed under running water)
Oil 5 tbsp
Garlic 1 tbsp (finely chopped)
Fresh red chilli 4 (finely chopped)
Oyster sauce 2 tbsp
Soya sauce 1 tbsp
Fresh basil (*tulsi*) leaves 15 (roughly chopped)

Method

- In a bowl, add the egg white, cornstarch and salt.
- Mix well and add the prawns.
- Allow to marinate for half an hour.
- Heat 3 tablespoons of oil.
- Pan fry the prawns, remove and keep aside.
- In the same pan, heat 2 tablespoons of oil.
- Add the garlic and fry till slightly golden brown.
- Add the red chillies, oyster sauce and soya sauce.
- Add the prawns to the sauce. Mix well.
- Add the basil leaves and toss everything together.
- Season with salt. Remember: sauces contain salt, so keep checking while adding more.
- Serve hot.

Fresh basil has a fantastic, sharp flavour that seamlessly blends with the rest of the spices. Important tip: make sure you don't overcook the prawns.

When you are in a mood to make a gourmet dish, do give this recipe a try. Your friends and family will be blown over once they dig in. You shall be applauded as a professional chef! The cheese gives it a soul-satisfying creaminess. Topped with nuts and basil, prawn tortellini with sun-dried tomato is a heavenly treat.

Prawn Tortellini with Sun-dried Tomato

Serves: 4

Ingredients

For the Prawn Filling

- Prawns 150 gms (deveined & washed)
- Garlic 1 tsp (finely chopped)
- Chilli flakes ½ tsp
- Cream 50 ml
- Ricotta cheese 50 gms (optional)
- Lemon juice ½ tsp
- Salt to taste

Other Ingredients

- All-purpose flour (*maida*) 200 gms
- Salt (a pinch)
- Egg 2
- Olive oil 1 tsp
- Water to sprinkle
- Oil 1 tbsp
- Garlic 1 tbsp (finely chopped)
- Chilli flakes ½ tsp
- Sun-dried tomatoes ½ cup (chopped)
- Cream 50 ml
- Basil (*tulsi*) leaves 10 (roughly torn)
- Pine nuts ¼ cup (roasted)

Method

- In a food processor, coarsely grind the prawns, garlic, chilli flakes and cream. Add the ricotta cheese, lemon juice and salt. Mix well and keep aside.
- In a bowl, add the flour, salt, eggs, olive oil and knead to make a stiff dough.
- Sprinkle a little water to bring the dough together. Cover with a moist cloth and keep aside to rest.
- Divide the dough and roll out into thin sheets.
- Using a round cookie cutter or a drinking glass, cut out 3-inch circles.
- Put about ½ teaspoon of the filling in the centre of the circle.
- Next, slightly wet the outside edge of the circle with water.
- Fold the circle to form a half circle and press the edges to seal.
- Hold the half circle at the corners. Take the outer corners and roll them around your thumb. Press the end and seal with some water.
- Place on a floured surface and repeat with the remaining rounds.
- In a large deep pot, boil the water with salt. Add the tortellini in batches, leaving enough room for the tortellini to be able to move freely in the boiling water.
- Boil the tortellini for about 5 minutes or until they float. Remove and keep aside.
- In a pan, heat the oil. Add the garlic and fry till golden brown.
- Add chilli flakes, chopped sun-dried tomatoes and cream.
- Add the cooked tortellini and toss lightly till the sauce has evenly coated the tortellini.
- Add the basil leaves and pine nuts. Serve.

Mixed Seafood Biryani

Serves: 6-8

Ingredients

Oil 1 cup
Green chilli 4 (slit)
Onion 4 (thinly sliced)
Ginger paste 2 tbsp
Garlic paste 2 tbsp
Tomato 2 (diced)
Fresh coriander (*dhania*) leaves 4 tbsp (finely chopped)
Mint leaves 20 (chopped)
Red chilli powder 1 tbsp
*Garam masala powder ½ tsp
Lemon juice extracted out of 2 whole lemons
Curd / yoghurt (*dahi*) ½ cup
Salt to taste
Prawns 500 gms (shell removed & deveined)
Seer fish 500 gms (cut into cubes)
Rice 3 cups (washed & soaked for 10 minutes)

Method

- In a heavy-bottomed pan, heat the oil. Add the green chillies and onions.
- Fry till the onions turn golden brown.
- Now, add the ginger-garlic pastes. Fry for a minute.
- Add the tomatoes, coriander and mint leaves. Cook till the tomatoes are soft.
- Add the chilli powder, garam masala powder, lemon juice, curd and salt.
- Cook this gravy till the oil separates.
- Add the prawns and fish cubes.
- Cook for 3 minutes and remove the pan from heat.
- In a large pot, boil the water. Add the rice and salt.
- Cook till the rice is ¾th done. Strain and keep aside.
- Layer the rice over the prepared seafood gravy.
- Cover and cook on low flame for 15 minutes or till the rice is completely done.
- Serve the biryani with pudina raita.

For the Pudina Raita

Cur / yoghurt (*dahi*) 100 gms (beaten)
Onion 2 (sliced)
Tomato 1 (chopped)
Cucumber 1 (chopped)
Mint chutney 2 tbsp (grind 25 gms mint leaves, 15 gms coriander leaves, 2 green chillies & ½ tsp cumin seeds into a smooth paste)
Salt to taste

Method

- In a bowl, mix all the ingredients well and serve with the biryani.

*For the garam masala powder recipe, refer to page no. 8

Try a medley of fish and other seafood varieties like scallops and squids, to make an exquisite platter of mixed seafood biryani. In this recipe, I have used a combination of fish and prawns. Team the dish with a bowl of pudina raita and indulge in the goodness of this one-of-a-kind seafood biryani. I have used Zeera Samba rice which is flavourful and aromatic; if not available, use any small-grain rice like Sona Masuri.

This sounds like such an exotic dish, but is really a rather simple one to make. I love risotto and always refer to it as the 'Italian khichdi'. The creamy risotto complements the fish well. The orange and dill sauce brings the zest and extra tang to the dish. I have used sea bass in this recipe, you can of course opt for your favourite fish.

Fish with Risotto and Orange Dill Sauce

Serves: 6-8

Ingredients

*Red chilli paste 2 tsp
Black pepper powder ½ tsp
Garlic paste 1 tsp
Lemon juice extracted out of 1 whole lemon
Salt to taste

Fish 500 gms (boneless fillets)
All-purpose flour (*maida*) ½ cup
Parmesan cheese ¼ cup (grated)
Oil 3 tbsp
Egg whites 2 (lightly beaten)

For the Risotto

**Chicken stock 1½ litres
Olive oil 3 tbsp
Onion 1 (finely diced)
Garlic 1 tsp (finely chopped)
Turmeric (*haldi*) powder ¼ tsp
Arborio rice 200 gms

Vinegar 1 tbsp
Butter 50 gms
Cream 100 ml
Parmesan cheese 2 tbsp (grated)
Parsley 3 tbsp (chopped)

Method

- In a bowl, add the chilli paste, pepper powder, garlic paste, lemon juice and salt. Mix well.
- Add the fish fillets and allow to marinate for half an hour.
- For the risotto, pour the chicken stock into a saucepan and bring to a boil. Simmer on low flame.
- Meanwhile, heat the olive oil in a large saucepan on medium flame.
- Add the onion and garlic. Sauté until the onion is soft.
- Add the turmeric powder.
- Add the Arborio rice to the onion mixture and cook, stirring for 2 minutes, until the grains appear glossy.
- Add a ladleful (1 cup) of the simmering stock to the rice mixture and stir constantly with a wooden spoon until the liquid is completely absorbed.
- Continue adding the stock, one ladleful at a time, stirring constantly and allowing the liquid to be absorbed before adding the next ladleful.
- Do this for about 15 minutes until the rice is creamy and tender, yet firm to the bite.

- Stir in the vinegar.
- Add the butter, cream, Parmesan cheese and parsley. Keep aside.
- In a large bowl, mix the flour and Parmesan cheese. Keep aside.
- In a grill pan, heat the oil.
- Dip the fish fillet in egg and then roll the fish with the flour and Parmesan mixture till the fish is coated evenly on all sides.
- Fry the fish for about 3 minutes till golden brown.
- To serve, heat the risotto and spoon on a serving plate, place the fish on it. Drizzle the orange and dill sauce over the fish.
- Serve with butter-tossed French beans.

*For the red chilli paste recipe, refer to page no. 9
**For the chicken stock recipe, refer to page no. 33

For the Orange and Dill Sauce

Butter 1 tbsp
Garlic 1 tsp (chopped)
Chilli flakes 1 tsp
All-purpose flour (*maida*) ½ tsp
Orange 1 (juiced)
Dill leaves 1 tbsp (finely chopped)
Salt to taste

Method

- In a pan, heat the butter.
- Add the garlic and fry till soft.
- Add the chilli flakes, flour and fry for half a minute.
- Add the orange juice, stir continuously and cook till the mixture slightly thickens.
- Add the dill leaves and cook for another minute.
- Season with salt.
- Keep aside till use.

Desserts

Mango Kheer 174

Crème Caramel 175

Creamy Milk Pudding with Chocolate Sauce and Almond Praline 176

Blueberry Cheesecake 179

Khoya Jamun 181

Anday Ki Mithai (Egg Halwa) 182

Tender Coconut Jelly with Coconut Cream 185

Gajari Spring Roll 186

Vermicelli and Date Squares 188

Molten Lava Cake 189

Chocolate Banoffee Tart 191

Khubani Ka Meetha (Apricot Trifle) 192

Shahi Tukda Fruit Bites 195

Gud Ka Paluda (Jaggery and Rice Pudding) 196

Tropical Fluff 198

Khajoor (Deep-fried Cookies) 199

Halwa Chonga (Fried Pastry Roundels) 200

Mango Kheer

Serves: 8

Summer is incomplete without the king of fruits, i.e. mango. Why not pair these juicy and sweet mangoes with rich creamy rice and seal a perfect ending to a lazy afternoon meal?

Ingredients

- Milk 1 litre
- Rice ¼ cup (washed & soaked for 2 hours)
- Sugar ¼ cup
- Cardamom (*elaichi*) powder ¼ tsp
- Ripe mangoes 250 gms (cut into small cubes)
- Pistachios 50 gms (roasted & chopped)

Method

- Boil the milk.
- Add the rice and cook till the rice is soft and starts to break up.
- Add the sugar and stir continuously until the kheer achieves a thick consistency.
- Once the kheer cools down, add the chopped mangoes and cardamom powder. Mix well and refrigerate.
- Garnish the kheer with pistachios and serve.

Crème Caramel

Serves: 8

Ingredients

- Sugar 1 cup
- Egg 5
- Condensed milk 1 cup
- Vanilla essence ½ tsp
- Milk 3 cups
- Cream 1 cup
- Lemon zest 1 tsp
- Fresh coconut 1 tbsp (grated & lightly dry roasted / optional)

Method

- In a saucepan, heat the sugar until melted, golden brown and caramelised.
- Pour the caramel evenly into the ramekins (approximately 9 ramekins).
- In a large bowl, whisk the eggs.
- Add the condensed milk, vanilla essence, milk and cream. Whisk well. Strain this mixture.
- Pour the mixture over the set caramel into the ramekins.
- Place the ramekins into a large baking tray.
- Pour enough boiling water into the tray to reach half way up the sides of the ramekins.
- Bake in a preheated oven at 180°C for 45 minutes till the custard has set.
- Refrigerate for about 5 hours or overnight.
- To serve, run a knife along the edge of the ramekin to loosen the sides of the custard.
- Invert on the serving plate. Garnish with lemon zest and grated fresh coconut.

There is nothing too fancy about preparing custard. The simplicity of this dessert wins hearts like no other. Treat your loved ones to crème caramel and make memories worth a lifetime.

Creamy Milk Pudding with Chocolate Sauce and Almond Praliné

Serves: 8-10

Ingredients

Milk 1 litre	Condensed milk 1 tin (400 gms)
China grass (*agar-agar*) 10 gms	Sugar 2 tbsp

For the Chocolate Sauce

Milk ¼ cup	Cocoa powder ¼ cup
Sugar ¼ cup	

For the Almond Praline

Sugar 3 tbsp	Almonds 15

Method

- Boil the milk and allow it to simmer.
- Soak the china grass in ½ cup of water for a minute, squeeze out excess water and add to the milk. Keep stirring for 5 minutes till the china grass dissolves.
- Add the condensed milk and sugar.
- On a medium-low flame, keep stirring and cook for about 10 minutes till the mixture slightly thickens.
- Strain and pour the milk mixture into the mould of your choice or a square tray. Refrigerate for 3 hours or till the pudding is set.
- To make the chocolate sauce, combine all the ingredients in a saucepan and whisk till combined.
- Boil the mixture, stirring continuously till the sauce thickens.
- Let the sauce cool down.
- To make the almond praliné, in a pan, add sugar and cook till caramelised.
- Add the almonds and cook for half a minute.
- Remove the mixture in a greased plate, allow to cool and crush coarsely.
- Spread the chocolate sauce over the pudding.
- Sprinkle the almond praliné for garnish. Serve.

This is one good-looking dish on the dinner table! The golden praline almonds sit so pretty on the pudding. And then, there is chocolate as well. You can never go wrong with chocolate. This pudding is certainly a must-try dessert.

Cheesecakes always look so complicated to make and can easily daunt a beginner. This is a cake that requires no baking. But that doesn't compromise on either the look or the taste of this dessert. Important tip: make the topping using fresh blueberries or fresh strawberries (when in season).

Blueberry Cheesecake

Serves: 8 pieces

Ingredients

Digestive biscuits 150 gms
Butter 50 gms (melted)
Cream cheese 300 gms
Castor sugar 50 gms
Whipping cream 150 ml
Lemon juice 1 tbsp
Canned blueberry topping 2 tbsp
Gelatin 1 tbsp (bloom the gelatin by adding 4 tbsp of water and keep aside for 2 minutes. Heat in microwave for 10 seconds till it melts)

For the Blueberry Topping

Canned blueberry topping 1½ cups
Mixed fruit juice 50 ml
Sugar 2 tbsp

Method

- Crush the digestive biscuits, add the butter and mix well.
- Put the mixture in a loose-based cake tin and press with the back of a spoon.
- Set the base in the fridge for 15 minutes.
- In a bowl, with an electric hand blender, whip the cream cheese with castor sugar.
- Add the whipping cream and whisk well.
- Add the lemon juice, blueberry topping and continue whisking the mixture till it slightly doubles in size.
- Add the melted, cooled gelatin and gently mix.
- Put the cheese mixture on top of the biscuit base and set for 2 hours in the fridge.
- In a pan, add the blueberry topping, fruit juice and sugar.
- Cook the mixture till thick. Keep aside to cool down.
- After the cheesecake has set, spread the blueberry topping on top of the cheese layer.
- Demould, slice and serve.

My grandmother used to make the best gulab jamuns. I remember how she would prepare batch after batch without a hint of fatigue and lovingly distribute them to all my relatives. She knew I loved them very much and always made sure I got a handful before anyone else. I understood then, how food brings everyone together during joyous occasions. While you get ready-to-mix packets of gulab jamun everywhere, there is nothing like making them from scratch.

Khoya Jamun

Serves: Makes 25 jamuns

Ingredients

Khoya 250 gms
All-purpose flour (*maida*) 50 gms
Egg 1 (lightly beaten, use only half the quantity)
Clarified butter (*ghee*) ½ tbsp
Baking soda (a pinch)

For the Sugar Syrup

Sugar 250 gms
Water 3 cups
Oil for frying

Method

- In a deep pot, add the sugar and water and bring to a boil till a syrup forms.
- When you stir the syrup with a spoon, and touch the spoon it should feel slightly sticky. This will take about 15 minutes on medium-high flame.
- Remove from heat and keep aside.
- Meanwhile, in a large bowl, combine the khoya with all the remaining ingredients.
- Mix well and knead until the dough has a pliable consistency.
- Make small balls out of the dough and then give each an oblong shape.
- In a deep pan/kadai, heat the oil on medium-low flame.
- Fry the khoya jamuns in batches until golden brown.
- Once done, remove from the pan and immediately add these to the syrup. Heat the syrup before you add the hot jamuns.
- Make sure the syrup remains hot throughout.
- Let the jamuns soak for 5 minutes.
- Gently remove them from the syrup and keep aside in a wide bowl.
- Repeat the same process for all the batches of fried jamuns.
- After all the khoya jamuns are soaked and removed into the bowl, heat the remaining syrup and pour over the jamuns.
- Serve.

Anday Ki Mithai (Egg Halwa) Serves: 10-15

Ingredients

Khoya 500 gms
Sugar 500 gms
Almonds ½ cup (boiled in water & skin removed)
Saffron (*kesar*) ¾ tsp (soaked in 2 tbsp of hot water)
Egg 12
Clarified butter (*ghee*) 1½ cup
Almond flakes / slivers ¼ cup

Method

- In a bowl, mix the khoya and sugar. Keep aside.
- In a mixer, blend the almonds and saffron into a smooth, fine paste.
- Add very little water to assist in grinding.
- In a large bowl, with an electric hand blender, whisk the eggs for 3 minutes until slightly frothy. Add the khoya and sugar mixture.
- Add the almond and saffron paste.
- Add the ghee and mix well into a smooth, thick and lump-free mixture.
- Use your hands to mix well.
- Pour the mixture into a lined square baking tray/tin.
- Bake in a preheated oven at 250°C for about an hour.
- During the last 5 minutes, sprinkle the almond flakes and bake until you get a golden brown crust.
- Let the halwa cool down.
- Cut into pieces and serve.

I always get a look of surprise when I serve this dish, because no one believes that you can make halwa from eggs. I have wonderful memories associated with this dessert. My mother-in-law taught me the basics of preparing this dish years ago. She was such an amazing teacher that I always get it perfect even now. Also, this recipe became quite popular during my days at a cooking reality show. Anday ki mithai is unique, rich in flavour and absolutely delicious.

Tender coconut water is not just healthy but also one of the best drinks to indulge in during summer. It fills you with nutrients and refreshes you after a hot day out. The creamy flavour of the coconut milk, paired with cold jelly, promises to be an excellent thirst quencher.

Tender coconut Jelly with coconut cream

Serves: 8

Ingredients

China grass (*agar-agar*) 10 gms
Tender coconut water 3 cups
Sugar 3 tbsp
*Fresh coconut milk 2 cups
Condensed milk ½ cup
Pomegranate seeds ½ cup (to garnish)
Mint leaves (a few to garnish)

Method

- Soak the china grass with tender coconut water for 10 minutes.
- Add the sugar and bring to a boil on low flame, till the china grass dissolves.
- Pour the mixture into a tray. Refrigerate and allow to set.
- In a separate bowl, mix the coconut milk and condensed milk. Refrigerate.
- Cut the set tender coconut into cubes.
- Pour the cold coconut milk mixture on the cubes. Garnish with pomegranate seeds and mint leaves.
- Serve.

*For the fresh coconut milk recipe, refer to page no. 9

Gajari Spring Roll

Serves: Makes 15 rolls

Ingredients

Carrot 250 gms (grated)
Milk ¼ cup
Sugar ½ cup
Condensed milk ¼ cup
Khoya 200 gms
Chopped nuts 3 tbsp (almonds, cashew nuts)
Clarified butter (*ghee*) 2 tbsp
Spring roll wrappers 10
Maida slurry (1 tbsp all-purpose flour {*maida*} + 5 tbsp water)
Oil for frying
Honey 2 tbsp
White sesame (*til*) seeds 1 tbsp (roasted)
Black sesame (*til*) seeds 1 tbsp (roasted)

Method

- In a pan, add the carrot and milk.
- Cook till the carrot is slightly tender.
- Add the sugar, condensed milk and keep stirring for 4 minutes.
- Add the khoya, nuts and ghee. Mix well.
- Cook till the halwa is dry.
- Remove in a bowl and allow the halwa to cool down.
- Spoon the halwa on one side of the spring roll wrapper.
- Fold the edges and roll tightly. Seal the ends of the roll with the prepared maida slurry.
- Follow the same process to make the remaining spring rolls.
- In a deep pan/kadai, heat the oil. Fry the spring rolls till golden brown.
- Brush these rolls with honey and sprinkle sesame seeds.
- Serve.

This dessert is a sweet twist to the savoury spring rolls. If you are a fan of rolls and gajar halwa, gajari spring roll is going to leave you craving for more.

Vermicelli and Date Squares

Serves: 10

Ingredients

Butter 200 gms (unsalted)
Fine vermicelli 200 gms (crushed into small pieces)
Soft dates 300 gms (pitted & finely chopped)
Almonds ½ cup (chopped)
Pistachios ½ cup (chopped)
Condensed milk 1 cup

Method

- In a pan, heat the butter.
- Add the vermicelli and sauté on medium-low flame for about 5 minutes.
- Add the dates along with half of the almonds and pistachios.
- Keep the remaining half for garnish. Sauté for 3 minutes till the nuts are roasted.
- Remove the pan from heat and stir in the condensed milk. Mix well.
- Grease a square baking tin / mould. Pour the mixture and evenly flatten.
- Sprinkle the remaining almonds and pistachios.
- Press gently and allow to cool down. Cut into squares and serve.

I call this the closest Indian version of baklava. The vermicelli and the dates guarantee an outburst of flavours. Rich in dry fruits, this is a very simple dish to master. You wouldn't be able to stop at just one helping.

Molten Lava Cake

Serves: Makes 5 cakes

Ingredients

Dark chocolate 120 gms (semi-sweet)
Egg 2
Sugar 70 gms
Butter 120 gms + for greasing the ramekins
All-purpose flour (*maida*) 70 gms (sieved)
Cocoa powder 2 tbsp (for dusting)

Method

- Melt the chocolate in a double boiler or a microwave.
- In a separate bowl, use an electric beater to whisk the eggs and sugar until light and fluffy.
- Once the chocolate melts, remove from heat and add the butter. Mix until the butter melts.
- Add the chocolate-butter mixture to the eggs slowly and mix.
- Add the flour and fold until well combined.
- Grease the ramekins on all sides with butter and dust with cocoa powder.
- Pour the cake mixture till about ¾th way full.
- Place the ramekins on a baking tray in a preheated oven and bake at 180°C for 15 minutes.
- Remove from the mould.
- Serve with ice cream.

You have to agree that every dessert that chocolate finds its way into, turns into a show-stealer. Molten Lava cake is sinful, decadent and has the most delicious gooey chocolate centre, doubling up the magic. What is not to love about this beauty?

It's raining chocolate! Add toffee and bananas into this fountain of happiness and you'll get a heady combination. A boon for all chocolate lovers! I suggest you caramelise the condensed milk tin a day before.

Chocolate Banoffee Tart

Serves: 8

Ingredients

Condensed milk 1 tin (400 gms)
Dark chocolate biscuits 250 gms (I have used Oreo. Remove the cream filling from the centre)
Butter 50 gms (melted)
Cream 150 ml
Dark chocolate 200 gms (semi-sweet & roughly chopped)
Ripe banana 2
Whipping cream 150 ml
Cocoa powder 1 tbsp (for dusting)

Method

- To caramelise the condensed milk tin, fill a large saucepan with water and bring to a boil. Place the unopened condensed milk tin, cover and let it simmer for 2 hours. (Ensure there is enough water to cover the tin, throughout the cooking process.)
- Crush the biscuits in a blender.
- Remove in a bowl and add the melted butter. Mix well.
- Press the mixture into the base and the sides of a loose-based pie tin / dish.
- Refrigerate for 15 minutes.
- Boil the cream, remove from heat and add the chocolate.
- Mix using a hand whisk till the chocolate has melted and a smooth filling has formed.
- Spread this over the set biscuit base. Refrigerate and allow to set for 2 hours.
- Slice one banana.
- In a bowl, remove ¾th of the caramelised condensed milk.
- Add the banana slices and gently mix.
- Spread this on the set chocolate base. Refrigerate for half an hour.
- Whip the cream till stiff and spread on the chilled condensed milk layer.
- Slice the remaining banana and arrange on the whipped cream layer.
- Dust generously with cocoa powder.
- Refrigerate and serve.

Khubani Ka Meetha (Apricot Trifle)

Serves: 8-10

Ingredients

Dry apricots (*khubani*) 300 gms (washed & soaked in 2 cups of water for 15 minutes)
Sugar 6 tbsp
Lemon juice ½ tsp
Milk 3 cups
Custard powder 3 tbsp
Whipping cream 100 ml

Method

- Pressure cook the apricots with the soaked liquid to make them soft and tender, approximately for 2 whistles.
- Once the pressure drops, open the lid of the pressure cooker and allow the apricots to cool down.
- Deseed them. Wash the seeds, crack and remove the almond from the centre. Dry roast them and keep aside for garnish.
- Squeeze the apricots to make a coarse paste.
- Transfer to the pan, along with the liquid.
- Add 3 tablespoons of sugar and cook, stirring continuously till the mixture achieves a thick, jam-like consistency.
- Add the lemon juice and cook for another minute.
- Remove from heat and refrigerate. Allow it to chill completely.
- Boil the milk and add the remaining 3 tablespoons of sugar.
- Mix the custard powder with some water to make a paste.
- Slowly stir in the boiling milk. Stir continuously to prevent lumps.
- Once the mixture thickens, cook on low flame for 4 minutes.
- Chill the custard.
- Whip the cream till stiff. Keep aside.
- To serve, in a tall glass, spoon the apricot compote, then add a layer of the chilled custard followed by another layer of compote.
- Pipe the whipped cream. Garnish with roasted almonds.

Here, the apricot compote is served with either custard, ice cream or cream. Usually, to make the compote, dry apricots are left to soak overnight. However, in this recipe, I have shared a quicker method to soften the dry apricots. Just pressure cook them!

My version of this traditional dessert includes fruits that lend versatility to each bite and balance the extra sweetness too.

Shahi Tukda Fruit Bites

Serves: 8-10

Ingredients

- Milk 500 ml
- Khoya 150 gms
- Condensed milk ½ cup
- Sugar 3 tbsp
- Butter 25 gms
- Light brown sugar 50 gms
- Cream 200 ml
- Bread 20 slices
- Oil for frying
- Assorted cut fruits to garnish (kiwi, fresh figs, cherries, plums, apples, grapes etc.)
- Whipped cream to garnish

Method

- In a pan, add the milk, khoya, condensed milk and sugar. Bring it a boil.
- Reduce the heat and cook till the mixture has thickened. Keep aside to cool down.
- To make the caramel sauce, melt the butter in a pan.
- Add the light brown sugar and cook until caramelised.
- Add the cream and cook till everything has combined together into a creamy sauce.
- With the help of a cookie cutter, cut the bread into circles or any shape of your choice.
- Fry these bread circles till golden in colour. Keep aside and allow to cool down.
- Dip the bread slices in the milk mixture.
- Spread the caramel sauce. Pipe the whipped cream.
- Garnish with fresh fruits.
- Serve.

Gud Ka Paluda (Jaggery and Rice Pudding)

Serves: 10-15

Ingredients

Coconut milk 800 ml
Rice ½ cup (soaked for 3 hours)
Jaggery (*gud*) 300 gms (grated or powdered & soaked in a little water)
Fennel (*saunf*) powder 1 tsp
Cardamom (*elaichi*) powder ½ tsp

For the Crumble

Clarified butter (*ghee*) 2 tbsp
Fresh coconut 1 cup (grated)
Groundnuts ½ cup (roasted & skin removed)
Sesame (*til*) seeds 2 tbsp

Method

- In a mixer, grind the coconut milk and rice until smooth.
- Strain through a muslin cloth.
- Add the soaked jaggery to this strained milk and mix well.
- Cook this mixture, stirring continuously to ensure there are no lumps.
- Cook on medium flame till the mixture thickens. It should start bubbling and leave the sides of the pan. This will take about 20-25 minutes.
- Add the fennel and cardamom powder.
- Spoon the mixture into silicone moulds or bowls. Allow to set in the fridge for about an hour.
- In a pan, heat the ghee.
- Add the grated coconut and fry till light golden brown. Be careful not to burn the coconut.
- Add the groundnuts and sesame seeds. Fry for half a minute and keep aside.
- Remove the pudding from the mould.
- Garnish generously with the crumble.
- Serve.

Every community has its own treatment of kheer or payasam. I have used canned coconut milk in this recipe. This pudding sets without any gelatin or agar-agar. Important tip: to achieve the right consistency, keep stirring continuously and do not lose patience.

Tropical Fluff

Serves: 8

Ingredients

Canned pineapple slices 1 tin (syrup strained & slices diced)
Canned cherries 1 tin (syrup strained & cherries cut into half, discarding the seed)
Gelatin 1 tbsp (add 2 tbsp of water & allow to bloom)
Condensed milk 1 tin (400 gms)
Whipping cream 200 ml
Icing sugar 3 tbsp

Method

- In a deep pan, add 1 cup of pineapple syrup and ½ cup of cherry syrup. Bring to a boil.
- Remove from heat and immediately add the bloomed gelatin. Stir till it dissolves completely. Allow to cool down.
- In a mixer, blend the condensed milk. Add the cooled syrup and blend again.
- Pour this mixture in glasses and add chopped pineapple and cherries. Keep some for garnishing.
- Set in the fridge for half an hour.
- Using an electric whisk, whip the cream with icing sugar till thick.
- Put the mix in a piping bag. Pipe on the set layer.
- Refrigerate for 2 hours. Garnish with the reserved chopped pineapples and cherries. Serve.

This dessert brings the taste of a tropical island. I have used canned pineapple and cherries in this recipe but you can try using different kinds of canned fruits also. Usually, people tend to discard the syrup in canned fruits but I have used both the syrup and the fruits in this recipe. Though it looks elaborate and beautiful, this dessert is fairly simple to make. This dish is a big hit among kids.

Khajoor (Deep-fried cookies) Serves: Makes 30 cookies

Ingredients

All-purpose flour (*maida*) 450 gms
Semolina (*sooji*) 120 gms
Sugar 400 gms
Poppy (*khus khus*) seeds 50 gms
Sesame (*til*) seeds 25 gms
Almonds 75 gms (chopped)
Cashew nuts 75 gms (chopped)
Dry coconut 1 cup (grated)
Fennel (*saunf*) seeds 1 tbsp (coarsely crushed)
Cardamom (*elaichi*) 2 pods (coarsely crushed)
Baking soda (a pinch)
Clarified butter (*ghee*) ¼ cup
Khoya 200 gms
Egg 2
Milk as required

Method

- In a large mixing bowl add flour, semolina, sugar, poppy seeds, sesame seeds, almonds, cashew nuts, grated coconut, fennel, cardamom, baking soda and mix till well combined. Keep aside.
- In a separate bowl add ghee, khoya and egg. Mix till combined.
- Add the khoya mixture to the flour mixture. Stir in milk accordingly and knead into a stiff dough.
- Divide the dough into 4 equal portions, sprinkle flour on the rolling board. Roll each portion into a circle / chapatti (1-inch thickness), using a knife and cut into diamond shape or any desired shape.
- In a kadai / deep pan, heat oil. Deep fry on medium heat till golden brown.

These are deep-fried cookies and can be stored in an airtight container for up to ten days. Khajoor cookies satisfy midday munchies, besides being an ideal tea time snack option.

Halwa Chonga (Fried Pastry Roundels) Serves: 20

Ingredients

For the Chonga

All-purpose flour (*maida*) 250 gms + 2 tbsp (for dusting)
Clarified butter (*ghee*) 2 tbsp (warmed)
Water as required
Oil for frying
Almonds 50 gms (blanched, skin removed & thinly sliced. Fry in 2 tbsp of clarified butter {*ghee*} and keep aside for garnish)

For the Halwa

Cashew nuts 100 gms (soaked in hot water)
Almonds 100 gms (blanched & skin removed)
Clarified butter (*ghee*) 2 tbsp
Cinnamon (*dalchini*) 1 stick
Bengal gram (*chana dal*) 2 tbsp (boiled & ground into a smooth paste)
Sugar 200 gms
Saffron (*kesar*) ½ tsp (soaked in 2 tbsp of warm water)

Method

- In a large bowl, add the flour and ghee. Mix well.
- Add the water as required and knead into a soft dough. Cover and keep aside. Divide the dough into 8 balls.
- Roll each ball into a thin chapatti. Ensure these are as thin as possible.
- Layer the 8 chapattis by drizzling some oil and dusting with little flour between each layer.
- Wrap all these layers into a Swiss roll. Cut this roll into small equal roundels.
- Gently roll each roundel into a small circle / chonga.
- In a deep pan / kadai, heat the oil. Fry these prepared chongas on medium flame.
- While frying the chongas, keep splashing a little oil carefully at regular intervals so that the layers separate. Fry till crisp and golden brown. Keep aside.
- Grind the cashew nuts and almonds into a smooth paste.
- To make the halwa, in a pan, heat the ghee. Add the cinnamon stick and Bengal gram paste.
- Fry on low flame for about 3 minutes or until the raw smell goes away. Add the cashew nuts and almond paste.
- Keep stirring and cook for 4 minutes. Add the sugar and saffron.
- Cook this mixture for 8 minutes till a thick consistency is achieved. Allow to cool down.
- Spread the halwa on the chonga. Garnish with fried almonds and serve.

To be honest, I have no idea how this dessert got its name. But halwa chonga is something I have grown up eating. I remember playing assistant to my grandmother in sprinkling the almonds and cashew nuts over the fried pastry roundels. This is a dessert I keep going back to and I would like you to create your own memories by perfecting the art of making these golden chongas.

Shazia

Acknowledgements

There are many people whom I would like to thank for being a part of my exciting culinary journey.

First and foremost, I am grateful to the Almighty for the wonderful opportunities in my life and for making my dreams come true.

I would like to dedicate this book to the memory of my beloved father, who always taught me to be happy under all circumstances and to make the best of every situation.

I would also like to thank:

My large-hearted grandmother, your inspiring presence in my formative years taught me to nurture my love of food and cooking;

My mother and my mother-in-law, you have been my guiding angels. Mumma, you brought me into this world and taught me the meaning of life and Mummy, you showed me the way to live;

My father-in-law, your advice and unconditional support have always driven me to strive for the best;

My sons, Aqeeb and Arzaan, you have been my biggest critics. You complete me;

My husband, Maqsood, your abundant love and unwavering encouragement have given me the strength to face all challenges;

My lovely family and amazing friends, your unconditional love and support motivate me. You all have been the wind beneath my wings;

Chef Sanjeev Kapoor, you have been my inspiration since childhood. Your shows have fuelled my passion for cooking;

Chef Vikas Khanna, you gave me the confidence to write this book;

Chef Ajay Chopra and Chef Kunal Kapoor, your invaluable guidance and wonderful companionship have always been comforting;

Chef Michael Swamy, dear friend, you have been extremely helpful and by my side at all times;

My team, your hard work and willingness to treat this book as your own have made me overcome all hurdles;

Saina Jayapal, your brilliant photography has made this book look beautiful;

Farrukh Shadab, your exceptional skill in food styling and Sarabjeet, your exquisite selection of the cover and section-opening pictures have immensely helped me sail through this project;

My kitchen staff, without your support, the cooking and photo shoot for this book would not have been possible;

Ajay Mago, Publisher, Om Books International, you gave me the platform to express my love for cooking and food;

Ipshita Mitra, my editor, you brought my debut cookbook to life;

And finally, to all my fans, you inspire my cooking every day!

Index